Learning Recorder

How to Play the Recorder
(Video Instructions Included)

Barton Press

Copyright © 2021 by Barton Press

ALL RIGHTS RESERVED

No part of this book may be reproduced, stored in a retrieval system, or transmitted in any form or by any means, electronic, mechanical, photocopying, recording, scanning, or otherwise, without the prior written permission of the publisher.

Limit of Liability/Disclaimer of Warranty: the publisher and the author make no representations or warranties with respect to the accuracy or completeness of the contents of this work and specifically disclaim all warranties, including without limitation warranties of fitness for a particular purpose. No warranty may be created or extended by sales or promotional materials. The advice and strategies contained herein may not be suitable for every situation. This work is sold with the understanding that the publisher is not engaged in rendering medical, legal or other professional advice or services. If professional assistance is required, the services of a competent professional person should be sought. Neither the publisher nor the author shall be liable for damages arising herefrom. The fact that an individual, organization or website is referred to in this work as a citation and/or potential source of further information does not mean that the author or the publisher endorses the information the individuals, organization or website may provide or recommendations they/it may make. Further, readers should be aware that websites listed on this work may have changed or disappeared between when this work was written and when it is read.

Table of Contents

Foreword 1

Recorder Background 4

Preparations 9

    Obtaining a Recorder 9

    Parts of the Recorder 10

    Assembling the Recorder 11

    Hand Position 12

    Posture 14

    Making Sound 14

Care and Maintenance 17

    Wooden Recorders 18

    Daily Care 18

    Monthly/Yearly Maintenance 19

    Additional Care Information 20

    Plastic or Resin Recorders 20

Basics of Music 22

The Musical Alphabet 22

Ledger Lines 26

Sharps, Flats, and Naturals 27

Timing, Counting, and Tempo 30

Pulse and Beat 30

Basic Notes and Rests 31

Meter, Measures, and Bar Lines 33

Pick-Up Notes 36

Rhythmic Dots and Ties 36

Additional Tempo Markings 38

Other Symbols and Markings 38

Recorders Tuned in "C" 41

Notes B-A-G 41

Reading a Fingering Diagram 44

Sharps and Flats 49

Advanced Techniques 53

Recorders Tuned in "F" 57

Reading a Fingering Diagram 59

Sharps and Flats 64

Advanced Techniques 68

Tone Quality and Tuning 71

Breath Control 71

Low vs. High Notes 74

Intonation 75

Scales and Key Signatures 77

Expression **82**

Dynamics 82

Vibrato 85

Articulation 88

Interpretation 91

Ornaments 92

Trills 93

Mordents 94

Glissando/Portamento 95

Additional Information **98**

Troubleshooting 98

Tips and Tricks 101

Solo Recorder vs. Duets, Trios, and Recorder Consorts 103

Daily Exercises and Routines 105

Posture and Hand Position 105

Breathing Exercises 106

Rhythm Exercises 107

Exercises and Songs for Recorders in "C" 109

Exercises for Recorders in "F" 114

Listening Suggestions 123

Recorder Virtuosos 123

Recorder Ensembles 123

Composers of Recorder Music 124

Recorder Websites 124

Afterword 127

Glossary 128

Helpful Videos

We've compiled a list of the most helpful Recorder video instructions for you!

Please visit:

activitywizo.com/rec

Foreword

Welcome to "Learning Recorder", a guide encompassing the basics for learning how to play the recorder. This informational guide approaches learning the recorder as a total beginner on the instrument. We discuss everything from what types of recorders you can purchase, how to assemble your recorder, how to take good care of it, and of course, how to make your first sounds and play music!

As you progress through this guide, you will learn about fundamental techniques used to play the recorder and encounter simple tunes where you apply these techniques. The essential elements of musical notation are also included to assist in learning how to read music. You may also wish to find and read a guide specializing in how to read music.

While this guide contains valuable information for any beginning recorder player, consider also finding a recorder teacher or mentor. A knowledgeable teacher will ensure that you are applying the information properly and making progress on your instrument. Their expertise will allow them to hear and see issues to be corrected as they arise in your playing to ensure good habits and technique are established from the start. With this guide and a trained teacher, you will be well-equipped to start playing the recorder. If you are a teacher reading this, you may also find this guide useful in your recorder studio to maintain a cohesive curriculum and approach for beginners.

Because there are various types of recorders, please review the background and preparations portions of this guide before beginning to play. The type of recorder you own or are considering for purchase, will influence what notes and fingerings to use. Once you've mastered one type of recorder, you may wish to branch out to others, but initially it is strongly recommended to focus on one instrument until proficiency is achieved. Most sections of this guide apply to any recorder, however, two sections are specialized; Recorders Tuned in "C" and Recorders Tuned in "F". If you are not certain of what type of recorder you have, consult a recorder specialist.

Additional tools that will aid in your learning are a metronome and a quality music stand. Metronomes are purchasable as a device, but there are also free smart phone applications and online metronomes, too. Music stands can be found at most music retailers in person and online.

At the conclusion of this guide are preliminary exercises and songs to put your acquired knowledge into practice. You are encouraged to use these in daily practice because knowledge builds throughout this guide. Also included at the end are fingering charts for quick reference that can be used with any music you wish to play.

Daily practice is essential to your success on any instrument. More practice tips are mentioned throughout the guide, but initially try to set aside 10-15 minutes per day for playing your recorder. Let's get started

Recorder Background

The **recorder** is a musical instrument categorized as an internal duct flute in the **woodwind** family. Woodwind instruments are the family of instruments that produce sound by blowing air into the instrument, with air being split by a sharp edge, such as a reed or other mouthpiece component. An internal duct flute is any flute with a whistle mouthpiece, like the recorder. These are also known as fipple flutes. What distinguishes the recorder from other types of flutes is the presence of a thumb hole and seven finger holes.

The very first recorder-like instruments date back to ancient times. These initial "vertical flute" instruments were primitive in nature and found in various areas around the world. The current-day recorder emerged in Europe in the Middle Ages, estimated around the 15th century during the Renaissances period. The "Golden Age" of the recorder is considered to be the Baroque Era, in the 17th to mid-18th century. Many prolific composers wrote solo music for the recorder during this time as well as ensemble music featuring the recorder.

After the Baroque Era, the recorder lost its popularity to the flute. It is important to note that until the invention of the modern-day concert flute (also called the transverse flute because it is played horizontally rather than vertically), the names "flute" and "recorder" overlapped as names for the recorder. In music prior to the 19th century, musical scores marked *flauto* referred to the recorder, whereas *flauto transverso* referred to the transverse flute.

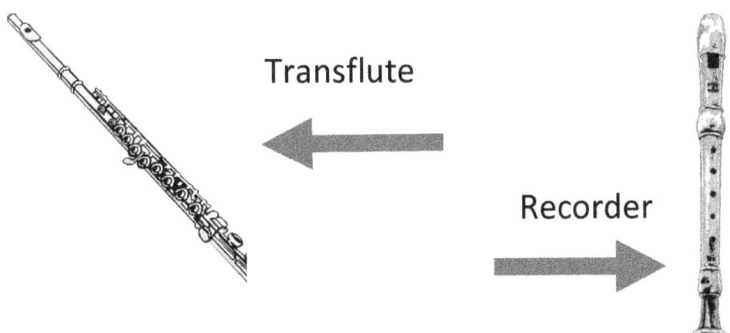

Although the recorder vanished for a time in music history after its Golden Age in the Baroque Era, it made a comeback about 150 years later. The instrument made a resurgence in the 20th century with the revival of Baroque music, and today is actively used in performances and educational programs. There are various types of recorders based on size, shape, and material. For this guide, we will discuss the most commonly played of today's modern recorders: the *sopranino, soprano, alto, tenor, and bass recorders*. Recorder sizes are named after vocal ranges in music and vary in range based on size. The sopranino recorder is the smallest and highest in range. It is about the size of a pencil and plays in the range of F5 to G7. The soprano recorder is next in size and has a sounding range of C5 to D7. The alto recorder has a range of F4 to G6, the tenor has a range of C4 to D6, and the bass recorder has a sounding range of F3 to G5. If you aren't familiar with the register system in music that uses letters and numbers to specify notes, don't worry. These letters and numbers refer to the letter name of a note and how high or low it is. In simple terms, this means that the lower numbers are lower notes, while the higher numbers are higher notes. For now, it is useful to know that the sopranino recorder is the highest in sound, followed by the soprano, then alto, then tenor, and then bass.

Recorder Ranges on the Treble Clef Staff

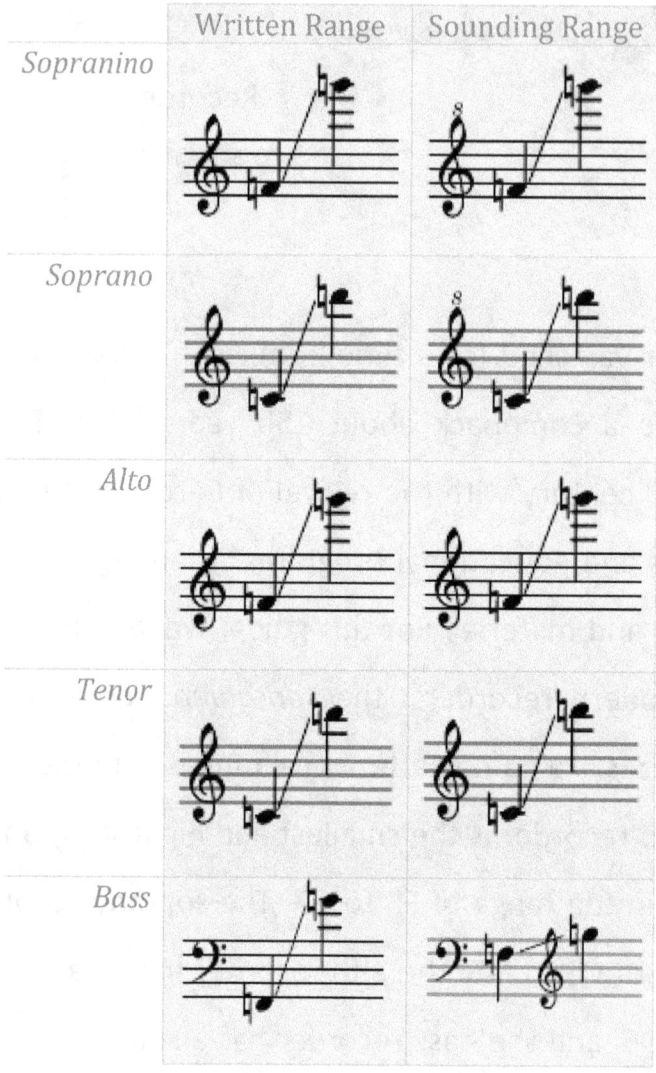

In the diagram above, the ranges of each type of recorder studied in this guide are shown on the treble clef staff. If you are not familiar with how to read notes on the treble clef staff, don't worry, the musical staff will be discussed later in this guide in the Basics of Music portion. The small number eight above the treble clef in the sounding pitches of the sopranino and soprano recorders indicates the notes shown are sounded an octave higher than where they are written. An octave is eight steps and contains the same letter names for the notes in question.

The material a recorder is made from varies as well. The most high-quality instruments are constructed of hardwoods and ivory, and will occasionally have metal keys rather than open holes. Mass manufacturers of recorders use plastic or resin, which is common for student level recorders because it is more durable and easier to upkeep. Resin and plastic recorders are also more modestly priced than wooden recorders.

In addition to various sizes and materials, it is possible for recorders to be of different varieties distinguishable by the design in relation to the tone holes. Distinguishable by the sizes of some of the tone holes, a recorder can be of the Renaissance style, Baroque style, or German style. Fingerings are simpler and more universal with the Baroque style recorder, and it is recommended to use a Baroque style recorder because of its consistency with, and application of fingerings, to other instruments, including all sizes of recorder. Most models of recorders are made in the Baroque style, so it is the standard. Recorders with German fingering are obsolete and manufactured for educational purposes exclusively. Renaissance recorders are useful when performing music of its time for the authenticity of the tone. Renaissance recorders have some limitations that Baroque recorders do not.

It is important to note that while the fingering systems are the same across all recorder types, the tuning can be in either "C" or "F". This means that when all of the holes are covered, a recorder tuned in C will sound the note "C", whereas a recorder tuned in F will sound the note "F" with the same holes covered. The most popular recorder, the soprano recorder, is tuned in "C". The soprano recorder will be featured first in this guide, along with the tenor recorder which is also tuned in "C". Most solo recorder music, however, is for the alto recorder. The sopranino, alto, and bass recorders, are all tuned to "F" and will also be explained in the "Recorders in "F" portion of our guide.

In most school programs, the resin/plastic variety of the soprano recorder are used because of their accessibility in size for small hands and fingers. Their durability and ease of care are also considerations when chosen for school programs and young students. These are great recorders to start with for beginners of any age, and the skills and techniques developed on a soprano recorder will translate to other members of the recorder family as well as additional woodwind instruments such as the clarinet, flute, saxophone, and oboe.

The alto recorder is also an excellent choice for beginners that have large enough hands to hold the instrument comfortably. Alto recorders can be found in resin/plastic if you prefer the durability and ease of care and maintenance.

Preparations

Obtaining a Recorder

If you have obtained a recorder prior to reading this guide, you will need to determine what type of recorder it is. It could be one of several different sizes, styles, and materials as previously described. It is best to take the recorder to an instrument specialist to get it professionally evaluated, adjusted, and/or repaired. You must know what type of recorder you are playing in order to begin learning to play. Perhaps you've already determined the details. It is still advisable to at least have it play tested by a professional to ensure the instrument is in proper working order.

Before purchasing a recorder, several factors should be considered when choosing the right recorder for you. For a new player, it is advised to begin on either the soprano or alto recorder. The soprano recorder is smaller and ideal for smaller hands, and is a popular choice for children. It is not exclusive to children however, and is a prominent instrument in Renaissance ensemble music. The alto recorder is more prominent in Baroque music and is featured mostly as a solo instrument. Players with smaller hands might find it difficult to begin on the alto recorder. Either is a fine choice for beginners as long as you can hold the instrument.

Once you've decided which size is best, the material will need to be chosen. Beginners are advised to purchase high-quality, plastic recorders for their durability and affordability. The "wood grain" plastic recorders made by brands such as Yamaha, Aulos, or Zen-on are most ideal because they offer a realistic grip that prevents the plastic from being slippery. If, through experience, you find that you enjoy and are committed to playing the recorder, you can upgrade to a more expensive, wooden recorder.

Wooden recorders offer a richer tone quality to the sound and allow you to play with more expression. Plastic is great for beginners though because of the affordability, durability, and ease of care.

As mentioned previously, recorders can be found as Baroque (sometimes called English), Renaissance, and German style. The style influences the finger system for each type of recorder. In modern times, the standard fingering is the Baroque fingering. It is best to avoid German fingerings because they are obsolete. Renaissance fingering is a sort of specialty that can be explored once you've started to master the Baroque recorder fingerings.

Based on the information above, it is advised to purchase either a soprano or alto, "wood grain" plastic Baroque recorder. Regardless of which recorder size you have chosen (alto or soprano), you can pick up playing additional recorders later. A majority of the following content is applicable to any recorder, with specifications mentioned.

Parts of the Recorder

Once a recorder has been obtained, examine it, and learn the parts. The top section of the recorder with the mouthpiece and window is called the **head joint**. The shaped part where the lips will be placed at the top is the **mouthpiece**, or **beak.** The **window** is the small, square opening below the mouthpiece with a ramp leading into the recorder. . The second piece, called the middle joint or barrel, has most of the **tone holes** of the recorder. Tone holes are the holes that the fingers will be placed over to create notes. The front of the barrel is where there are multiple tone holes, with a double tone hole at the bottom of the column. The back is distinguished by the single tone hole at the top. The bottom portion is called the **foot joint**. It has a slight flair to it and is often called the bell because of the shape. There is also a double tone hole on the foot joint.

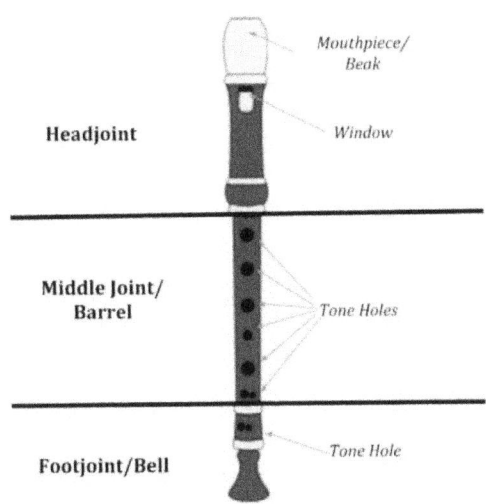

In the diagram above, the dark, horizontal lines represent where the head joint, middle joint, and foot joint are divided. Before assembling, we need to determine if your recorder is in three parts or two parts. Recorders can be two-jointed with a separation between the head joint and body, or three-jointed with a separation between the head joint, body, and foot joint. The latter is preferable because of its ability to adjust the bottom section to reposition the bottom tone hole in a way to make it more accessible for the pinky finger of the right hand.

Assembling the Recorder

When assembling either the two-jointed or three-jointed recorder, you can start with the head joint and body. For the two-jointed, these are the only two parts to assemble. Take the head joint and gently twist it into the barrel, using a gentle twisting motion rather than straight on to avoid exces tension that could cause damage to the seal or cork. Remember, the head joint is where the lips will be placed on the beak, and it has a square shaped window on the front. When handling the head joint, it is important that you do not press into the window of the recorder. The edge on the inside of the window, called the **labium**, is very delicate and if damaged will result in your recorder not being playable.

The front of the barrel has multiple tone holes, and the top of the barrel is where the single tone hole is on the back. The window of the head joint should align with the column of tone holes along the front of the body, and the single hole on the back of the barrel should be at the top, near the head joint.

Depending on the recorder, the **tenon joint** of the barrel may have a cork, or it may not. Wooden recorders often have a cork. The cork ensures that the parts of the recorder seal, so there aren't air leaks. If there is resistance in joining the parts, you may need to oil or grease the cork/tenon joints. See recorder maintenance and care on (page 16) for more information on cork grease and maintenance. Never force the parts together if there is resistance.

Once the head joint and barrel are properly aligned, a two-jointed recorder is assembled. The final piece for the three-jointed is the foot joint. This goes on the bottom of the barrel, with the flare at the very bottom, and the double tone hole aligned near the tone holes are on the barrel, or middle joint. The foot joint can be adjusted slightly off center to accommodate the pinky of the right hand which is discussed more in the following section.

Hand Position

Now that your recorder is assembled, we need to establish proper placement of your hands and fingers. Regardless of which hand is dominant, the left hand will always be the top hand. Each finger is assigned a tone hole, and in modern terminology, the holes and fingers are labeled zero through seven. On the left hand, the thumb is 0, index finger is 1, middle finger is 2, and the ring finger is 3. The pinky finger of the left hand doesn't have a number because it will not be used for a tone hole.

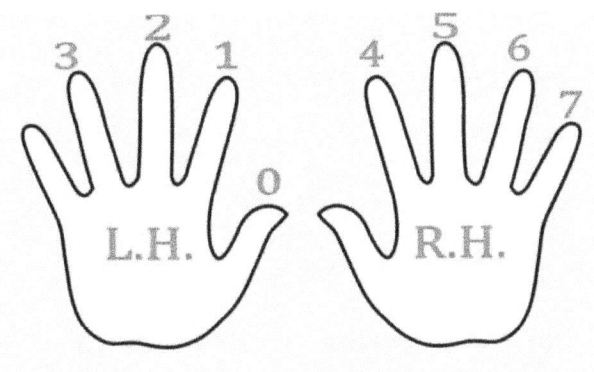

On the right hand, the thumb is not numbered, because it will not be used for a tone hole. The index finger is 4, middle finger is 5, ring finger is 6, and the pinky finger is 7. The tone holes of the recorder are numbered in correspondence with the finger numbers. The single tone hole on the back is 0, and on the front, the tone holes are numbered 1 through 7 from top to bottom.

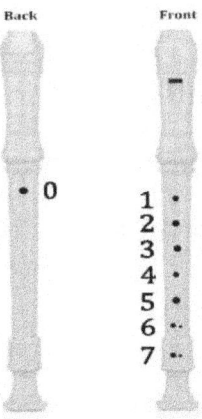

Fingers are assigned these tone holes exclusively and are not to be shifted around. Tone holes are covered and uncovered in various combinations to create different pitches or notes. When holding the recorder to play, the right thumb should be placed on the back of the recorder behind tone holes 4 or 5. The rest of your fingers should be aligned with their corresponding tone holes. To get used to holding the recorder, cover all of the tone holes with your fingers in the correct placement. If you have a three-jointed recorder, you can adjust tone hole 7 by turning the foot joint toward your right hand. Now, place the beak of the recorder between your lips. Do not bite with your teeth at all. Practice balancing the recorder to prepare for playing.

Posture

When preparing to play any instrument, it is essential to establish good playing posture. For a wind instrument like the recorder, this will allow for greater control of the diaphragm in regard to breathing. If choosing to stand while playing, stand with your feet approximately shoulder width apart. If you prefer sitting, sit toward the front of the chair with your feet planted firmly on the ground. Whether seated or standing, the back, neck, and head should be erect, shoulders back and relaxed, and the chin should be level with the ground.

Once you have your sitting or standing posture established, double check that you've also placed your fingers on the recorder properly. To achieve good balance between the hands, make certain the right thumb is behind tone hole 5. The elbows should be away from the body rather than tucked in, while remaining relaxed. The wrists of each hand should be straight and not bent. In general, it is best for the hands, wrists, and elbows to be in a natural position, with a straight flow from the elbows to the tips of the fingers.

Good posture is one of the most essential basics that will affect your playing. Poor posture is a difficult habit to break, so establish good posture from the start and set it each time you play.

Making Sound

When preparing to play any instrument, it is essential to establish good playing posture. For a wind instrument like the recorder, good posture will allow for greater control of the diaphragm in regard to breathing. If choosing to stand while playing, stand with your feet approximately shoulder width apart. If you prefer sitting, sit toward the front of the chair with your feet planted firmly on the ground. Whether seated or standing, the back, neck, and head should be erect, shoulders back and relaxed, and the chin should be level with the ground.

Now, in this posture, let's practice proper breathing technique. When playing a wind instrument, it is essential to learn to control the breath with the diaphragm rather than the chest or shoulders. Place your hands on your stomach. Practice inhaling slowly, focusing on the area beneath your hands and ensuring the shoulders remain relaxed and still. The area beneath your hands should expand slowly as you inhale each time. Do this several times, focusing on the diaphragmatic breathing. To play the recorder, a large volume of air is not necessary, so focus more on where you are sending the breath and not as much on bringing in a large quantity of air. It is best for air to be "on the move" and not stagnant. Inhaling too much air will cause stagnancy.

Once you've mastered the inhalation technique, practice exhaling with a steady airstream for five seconds. Then try extending the exhalation beyond five seconds while maintaining a steady stream of air. Inhaling with the diaphragm and controlling the rate of exhalation is what is needed to play a wind instrument like the recorder. It may take a few attempts to get the air speed and pressure consistent, but with deliberate practice, you will become proficient.

We are now ready to try blowing air into the recorder to create our first sounds. For now, simply place your left thumb over the back tone hole, #0, and your index finger on the top tone hole in front, #1. Place the beak of the recorder between your lips and gently seal your lips around the beak. The recorder should not touch your teeth. If it helps, you may place your right thumb on the back of the recorder behind tone holes

4/5 for balance assistance, but do not cover any additional tone holes. The recorder should be held at approximately a 45-degree angle from the body.

Breathe from the diaphragm, and exhale gently into the recorder. If you get no sound, try blowing slightly harder or faster. If you get a very sharp, high pitched, unpleasant sound you are blowing to hard or fast. The correct amount of breath pressure will produce a pleasant, steady, smooth sound. The recorder sounds best when played with a gentle air stream and low pressure. Do this several times to experiment in finding the correct amount of breath pressure. The goal is a steady, pleasant sound without any screeches.

Once a steady, pleasant sound is achieved, we are ready to add **articulation**. Articulation on the recorder is using the tongue to start each note. Say the word "du", observing where the tongue hits the roof of the mouth. We will use this release of the tongue from the roof of the mouth to separate notes. Holding the recorder in the same position as before with tone holes zero and one covered, try starting the sound with the "du" tongue action. This time, "du" will not be spoken. The tongue will make the same stroke followed by air into the recorder. Once the tongue releases from the roof of the mouth, immediately blow air into the recorder. Be careful to not get forceful, lest you get that high-pitched, unpleasant sound, from overblowing. Keep the air stream gentle and steady. After successfully articulating a few long tones, try to articulate four times within one breath. Once you're able to make a pleasant sound and use your tongue separating notes cleanly, you are ready to begin learning to play notes and make music!

Care and Maintenance

Caring for your recorder will prolong its use and maintain its playability over time. There are a few tasks that should be routinely completed for all recorders to keep them clean and ensure the highest quality of sound production. Wooden recorders require more care and attention over resin or plastic recorders. Be sure to refer to your recorder owner's manual for any specific instructions about caring for and storing your instrument.

Before getting started, there are a few more specific parts of the recorder you need to be aware of that may be involve in maintaining the instrument. First is the block. The block is the wooden piece where your bottom lip rests on the mouthpiece. It is made to absorb moisture, and it would be detrimental to your instrument for it to be submerged in water or oiled. You will also see the windway and bore referred to in this section. The windway is the opening at the top where your wind passes is blown into the instrument. The bore is the inside of the body of the instrument, like a tube, below the window of the recorder.

The image below is a diagram of a recorder from the side, with the mouthpiece facing to the left. Letter A is the block, letter B is the windway, letter C is the window, and letter D is the bore.

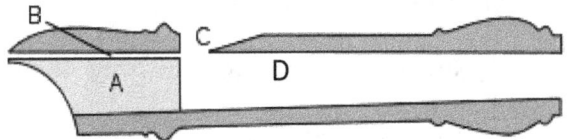

Wooden Recorders

New wooden recorders will have to be "broken in" by limiting the amount of time the recorder is played within the first month. Because the wood is new, the moisture produced when playing may strain the wood and cause cracking. This is because the wood on the inside that is exposed to moisture from our breath will expand, while the exterior stays dry. By gradually introducing moisture to the instrument, you will prevent the recorder from cracking. Recommendations of playing time vary by instrument size and creator, so be sure to refer to the instructions from the maker of the recorder. Many manufacturers instruct to play no more than 10-15 minutes per day for the first two weeks, 20 minutes per day in the third week, 25 minutes in the fourth week, and continue increasing by five minutes per day. After breaking in the recorder, it is still advisable to not play it for more than two hours on any given day. Many recorder makers will also recommend that you bring the instrument back to them following the initial "break in" period for necessary adjustments. If you own a used recorder and it has not been played for several months or years, it will need to be broken-in again.

It is best to establish daily, monthly, and yearly routines to maintain your recorder. Listed next are your daily maintenance routines for before, during, and after playing a wooden recorder. Remember to also refer to your specific instrument maker's instructions for specific instructions for caring for your instrument.

Daily Care

Before playing, it is advisable to wash your hands and brush your teeth. We do not want any food particles to be blown into the instrument, and clean hands will aid in maintaining the exterior of the instrument. It is also essential to warm up your recorder before playing it. Do this by holding the recorder close to your body or wrapping your hands around the instrument. A warm recorder will handle the condensation produced by playing more easily, which is important in preventing excessive clogging in the airway.

While playing your recorder, water will accumulate and sometimes cause the recorder to clog. This excess moisture will need to be cleared when this occurs. There are a few ways to clear a clog. One way is to take the head joint separately, close the end with the palm of your hand, and blow hard through the window of the head joint. Be careful not to touch the sharp edge of the window, called the labium. Doing so when the labium is moist may warp the wood and cause serious damage to your instrument. Clogs can also be cleared by covering the window with the palm of your hand and blowing sharply into the mouthpiece, or beak, of the recorder.

After playing your recorder for any length of time, leave the instrument out of the case so it can dry out. There is debate on whether it is necessary to swab out the inside of the recorder with a cleaning cloth. Most players only use a **cleaning rod** with cloth if the recorder is very wet. If using a cleaning cloth, be sure that it is lint free to prevent anything catching inside your recorder. Also be very careful not to poke the labium with the end of the cleaning rod. Never use rods with sharp edges or pointy ends. It may also be helpful to dismantle the recorder, especially if it has a cork, so that the cork can dry out. The instrument can be stored in the case once it has completely dried. Storing the instrument in the case while moist may cause molding.

Monthly/Yearly Maintenance

Should your wooden recorder require a deep cleaning at any point, it can be washed using lukewarm water containing dish detergent. It is best to remove the **block** when submerging the instrument in water. Removing the block may be difficult, and many players opt to take their instrument to a professional for yearly cleaning and maintenance. To wash without removing the block, use a lint free cloth with water and detergent and gently wipe the outside of the instrument.

Many recorder makers recommend oiling the **bore** (inside) of the recorder at least once per year. The type of oil to be used differs by manufacturer and should be included with the care instructions for your instrument. Oiling requires specific materials and may be best left to professionals initially until you've studied how to oil your specific instrument. The type of oil recommended is debated between professionals and can vary depending the type of wood from which your recorder is constructed.

Additional Care Information

Whether in or out of the case, avoid storing your recorder in direct sunlight. Keep your instrument in a well-regulated, temperament room that is neither too dry nor too humid.

If you ever have difficulty assembling or disassembling your recorder, the tenons may need greased. The **tenon** is where the individual joints of the recorder come together, or insert around/into each other. The tenons sometimes dry out or expand and need grease to allow for smooth assembly. You should not need any excessive force to assemble your recorder, and doing so may cause damage to the instrument. Simply grease the tenons slightly, wiping off any excess grease with a clean cloth. Very little grease is required. The type of grease recommended for your instrument varies. Refer to your instruments maker or a recorder professional to assess what type of grease is best for your instrument.

Plastic or Resin Recorders

Plastic recorders are very low maintenance. Keep the joints lightly greased, and wash out the recorder frequently so that nothing builds up in the windway or the bore. You can use soap or a mild detergent with lukewarm water and wash the instrument by hand. Be mindful of not damaging the labium just like with wooden recorders. When using a cleaning rod, be very careful not to scratch the inside of the bore, and like wooden recorders, never use anything with sharp or pointy edges and ends.

Basics of Music

When learning to play an instrument, it is recommended to also learn to read music. While it is possible to create music and play songs by ear (meaning just by hearing what you play), learning to read music will allow you to learn songs more quickly and become a more complete musician. This chapter will take an initial glance at how to read recorder music.

The Musical Alphabet

First, music written for any instrument uses the first seven letters of the English alphabet, "A", "B", "C", "D", "E", "F", "G". These letters are assigned to the notes that we will play. There are more than seven notes possible, however. The musical alphabet repeats itself as notes ascend or descend in relation to each other. For example, if a note were to be one step higher than "G", it would be an "A". One step higher than that "A" would be "B".

To get a complete understanding for how this applies to the recorder, here is the musical alphabet sequence for a recorder tuned in "C". On the far left is the lowest "C" possible on a recorder tuned in "C". Notice that the alphabet continues going forward as the notes get higher in pitch.

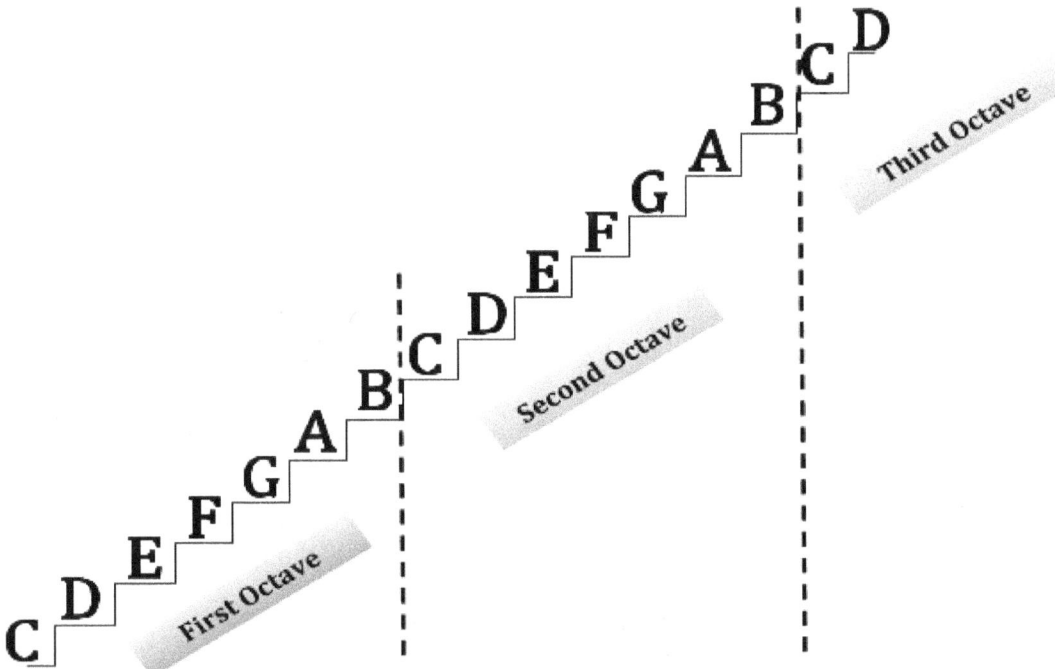

There are three different "C's" possible on recorders tuned in "C", three different "D's", and duplicates of the other letters also. Those notes that share the same letter name share a special relationship in sound, and on the recorder, oftentimes share similarly fingerings. The term **"octave"** is used most often to distinguish which note is being discussed when there are multiple of the same letter. An octave is the measurement of eight steps between notes, or eight notes apart. Looking at our sequence of letters above, count the first C on the left as number one. The following C will be number eight. These notes are an octave apart from each other.

The three different "C's" are used to group notes together into a three octave classification. The first seven notes are categorized as the first octave, because they are the lowest. The following C-D-E-F-G-A-B are the second octave notes, in the middle. And the final C and D, considered the third octave notes, are the highest on a recorder tuned in "C".

The same grouping of octaves is used for Recorders tuned in "F" as well. Rather than "C" being the lowest note, "F" is the lowest note, and it is used to group the notes into their three octave categories.

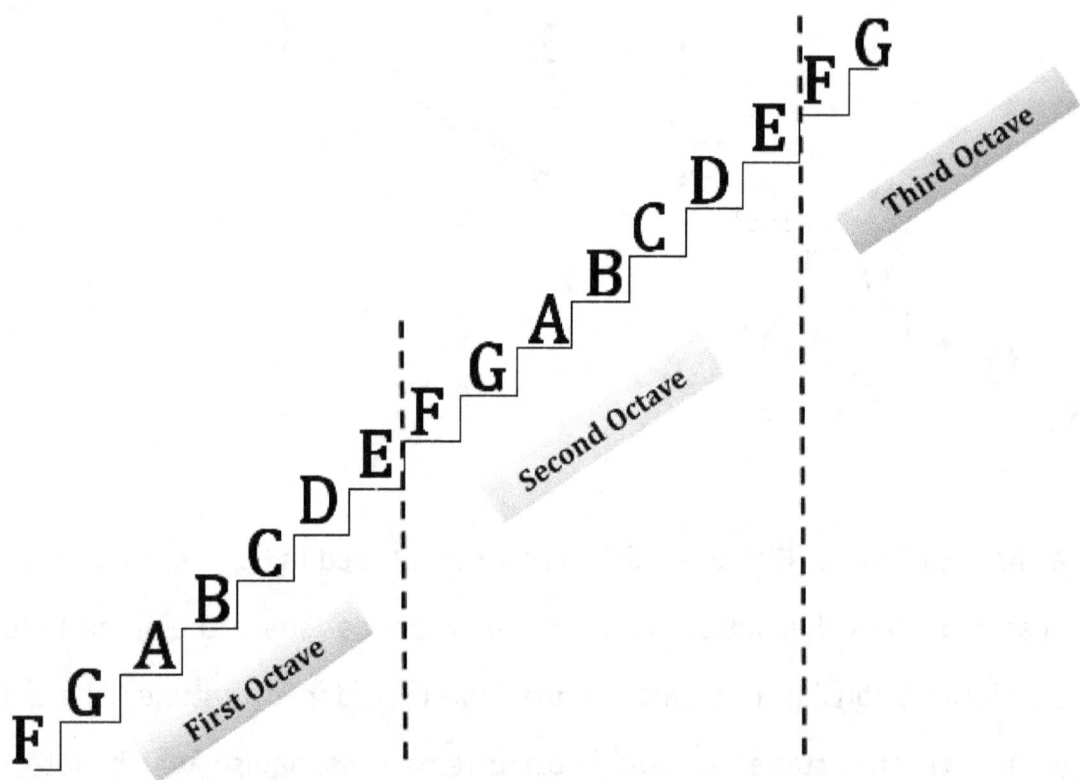

Now that we've established our musical alphabet, let's examine how this is notated into sheet music. Music is traditionally notated on five lines and four spaces. This is called a **staff**.

The Staff

On any staff, the lines and spaces between the lines are numbered from bottom to top. These numbers are used to refer to location on the staff. For example, if a note were to be on the bottom line, it would be on line 1. If a note were to be in between the bottom two lines, it would be on space 1. Each line and space are assigned a specific letter name that represents a particular note. For recorder, the **treble clef ($)** is used to designate these letters. The treble clef is found at the beginning of every piece of recorder sheet music. The notes represent specific pitches, and their letter names are notated beneath each note. The first five notes are the line notes in treble clef. The last

E G B D F   F A C E

four notes are the space notes in treble clef. The lines and spaces are lettered from bottom to top on the staff. In the treble clef staff, the lines are E-G-B-D-F, and the spaces are F-A-C-E.

Notice that when sequencing the letters from bottom to top, line to space, the staff is musically alphabetical. "E-F-G-A-B-C-D-E-F"

Notes that are higher in pitch will be toward the top of the staff, and notes that are lower will be toward the bottom of the staff. Because the music alphabet uses seven letters and then repeats itself in the same order, there are multiple notes of the same letter name. These are considered to be of the same pitch class, and are an octave apart. The notes above are the only notes to learn on recorder, they are our starting point for reading music in the treble clef, which the recorder uses.

Notes can expand above and below the staff as well. For example, a note can be written directly below the bottom line of the staff. This would be an additional note lower than the bottom line "E". Because the note is descending, it will be back one letter from "E" in the musical alphabet. In the sequence of the musical alphabet, this note would be a "D". It is considered a space note.

D

A note can also be written above the top line of the staff. This note would be a space note one step higher than the top line "F". This time, the alphabetical sequence is ascending, or going forward, so a note on the space right above the staff is a "G".

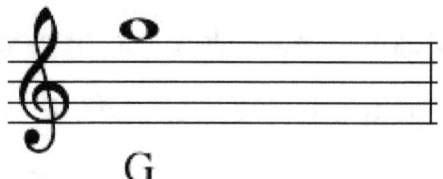
G

Ledger Lines

Ledger lines are short, individual lines used to expand the lines and spaces of the staff higher and lower than the primary five lines and four spaces. A ledger line is a temporary line used for the notes that extend lower than the bottom line or higher than the top line of the staff. The treble clef staff is five lines and four spaces, which offers nine total places for pitches from the musical alphabet to be notated. As mentioned in the previous section about the musical alphabet and staff, the bottom line of the treble clef is "E" and the space beneath the "E" line is used to notate the note "D". We can step down again by adding a short, individual line under the staff to notate the note "C". This short line is our first ledger line below the treble clef staff.

Additional ledger lines are added to notate notes lower than "C" on the treble clef, however this "C" is the lowest note within practical range on any recorder, specifically recorders tuned in "C".

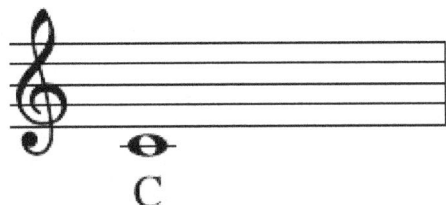
C

Ledger lines are also used to expand above the staff. The top line of the treble staff is "F", the space above "F" is "G". A ledger line can be added above the staff to notate the note above that space "G" at the top. This note would be "A". On recorders tuned in "C", the highest ledger line note is the "C" notated two ledger lines above the staff. Notes can also be notated in the spaces between the ledger lines, and the highest space note on recorders tuned in "C" is the "D" above the second ledger line above the staff.

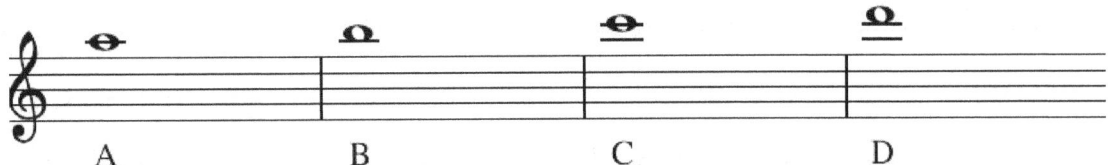
A   B   C   D

The lowest note on recorders tuned in "F" is the first space of the treble clef staff, "F", so there won't be any ledger lines below of the staff in music for sopranino, alto, or bass recorder. There are more notes possible that are notated above the staff. The highest ledger line note on recorders in "F" is notated on the fourth ledger line above the staff. This is the highest note in the range of these recorders.

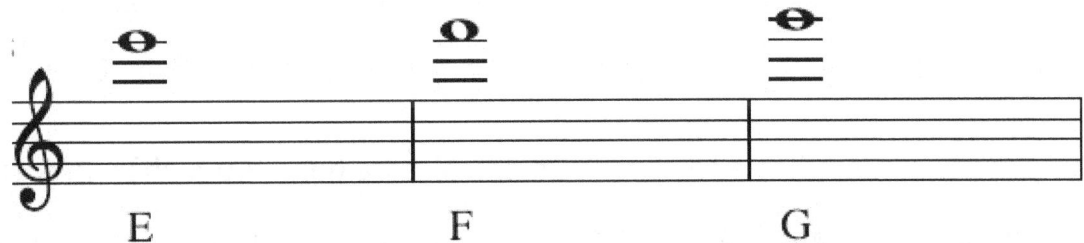
E   F   G

Sharps, Flats, and Naturals

When a note progresses from one to the very next, it can be measured as a step. Steps can be classified as whole steps or half steps, depending on the distance between the notes in question. In the musical alphabet, the letters are all considered natural notes.

There is a whole step between most of the natural notes, with the exceptions being "B" to "C" and "E" to "F". This is best visualized with the piano keyboard. The white keys are the natural notes, and in between most of these notes are black keys. The few places where there are no black keys are between all of the "B's" and "C's", and "E's" and "F's".

Pitches that are directly next to one another are considered to be a half step apart. On the piano keyboard, this can be from a black key to a white key, vice versa, or between the two white keys of the exceptions mentioned that have no black keys between them. This applies to the recorder because those black keys are additional notes between the other natural notes of the musical alphabet. These "in-between" notes are new pitches that will require new fingerings from the natural notes. They are basically the halfway point between the letters of the musical alphabet. For example, there is a note that is a half-step higher than "A", which is also a half step lower than "B". In any music, there are symbols used to indicate for a pitch to be a half step higher or a half-step lower.

A **sharp sign** is used to indicate for a note to be raised a half step higher. A note with a sharp sign will sound a half step higher than the natural pitch and is a half-step in pitch to the next note. A half step higher than "A" is "A sharp", or "A♯".

A **flat sign** is used to indicate for a note to be lowered a half step. A note with a flat sign will sound a half step lower than the natural pitch to which it is attached. A half-step lower than "A" is "A flat", or "A ♭".

♭

When notated in music, flats and sharps always carry through the measure to any notes of the same pitch class, or letter name. This means that if there were an "A♯" at the beginning of a measure, all "A's" would be sharp until the end of that measure. There is an exception to this rule - the **natural sign**. A natural sign is used to cancel a flat or sharp sign either within the same measure, or to cancel a sharp or flat in a notation called the key signature. Key signatures will be discussed in further detail later on in our guide. For now, get familiar with the flat, sharp, and natural signs and their meanings.

Because sharp and flat named notes (black keys on piano) are between the natural notes (white keys on piano), there are two names for the same pitch. This is demonstrated in the piano keyboard image below. A half-step above "C" is "C♯", a half step below "D" is "D♭", and this is the same pitch. This means there are two names for the same pitch. These are considered to be **enharmonic** equivalents. In this guide, both the flat and sharp name will be included when discussing these notes on the recorder.

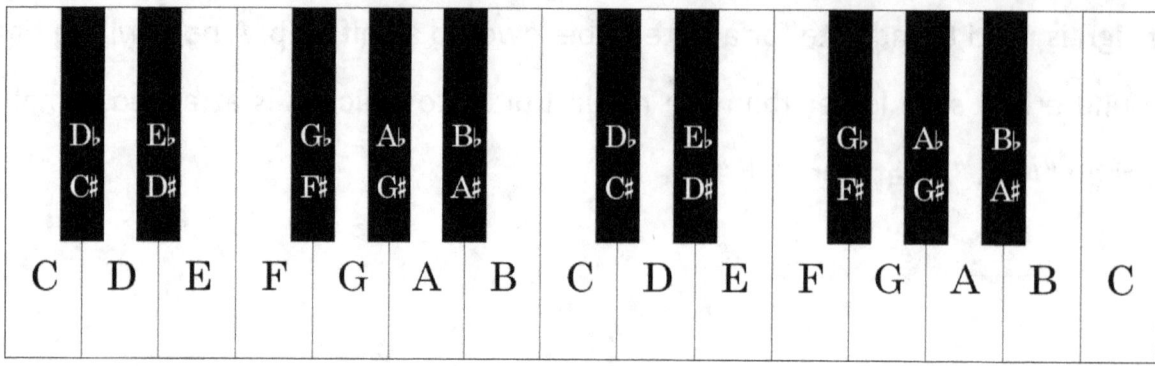

Timing, Counting, and Tempo

In music, timing and counting refers to the durations of sounds and how they are sequenced to create **rhythm**. Rhythm is the systematic arrangement of musical sounds that creates patterns in times. Musicians have to learn to count rhythms and beats in order to read music notation. Before examining rhythms and durations of notes, we first need to establish the musical pulse

Pulse and Beat

The pulse of music is much like the pulse of a heartbeat. Both beat at a constant, steady rate. The rate can be faster or slower, but once the rate is established, it should continue steadily at a constant speed. If you've ever caught yourself tapping your foot or nodding your head along with a favorite song, you were likely feeling the pulse of the music with your body. Many describe this as "feeling the beat", since the terms pulse and beat are basically interchangeable.

In order to properly train how to keep a steady pulse or beat, many instructors and students use an apparatus called a **metronome**. A metronome is a tool that produces an audible sound, such as a click or beep, and ideally a synchronized visual motion component, like a pendulum or a blinking light. Tapping or clapping with the metronome will train the ears and body to hear and feel a steady pulse. They are available in multiple formats such as physical devices (purchasable online and at local music retailers), interactive online metronomes, and even as applications for smart phones. Every aspiring musician should obtain a metronome.

In music, the speed of the pulse is called the **tempo**. Music can have a fast tempo or a slow tempo, and many tempos between and beyond fast and slow. Metronomes have the ability to set the speed of the audible tick or beep in accordance with the tempo desired using a system of numbers. The number system a metronome uses is called "Beats Per Minute", abbreviated "BPM". BPM measures how many beats are occurring within 60 seconds, or one minute. A BPM of 60 would be equal to the rate of a second, because there are 60 seconds in a minute. The higher the number, the faster the beat, and the lower the number, the slower the beat.

If music has a metronome marking, it will be pictured like this:

$$\quarternote = 80$$

The symbol on the left side of the equal sign is a duration of sound that will be examined later in this portion of the guide. For now, it represents a beat of sound, so in this metronome marking, the desired rate is 80 BPM, or Beats Per Minute.

Basic Notes and Rests

The appearance of a note beyond its location on the staff indicates its duration. Notes can be held out for longer or shorter durations by continuing or stopping the air stream while playing. For this guide, we are going to briefly examine the most basic elements of timing and counting.

When discerning the duration of a note, the information lies in whether there is a stem, if the note head is empty or solid, and if there is a stem or beam attached to the stem.

For this guide, you will need to identify and count **whole notes, half notes, quarter notes**, and **eighth notes**. For each note that includes a stem, the stem can face up or down. Both versions are included in the chart below.

Note Image	Name	Duration
𝗼	Whole note	4 counts
𝅗𝅥 𝅗𝅥	Half note	2 counts
♩ ♩	Quarter note	1 count
♪ ♪	Eighth note	½ count

Initially, practicing music that uses only whole, half, and quarter notes is recommended for beginners. Once coordination and fluency on these notes is established, music that includes eighth notes can be started. A single eighth note has a solid note head with a tail/stem/flag. It is counted for half of a beat, so it is shorter in duration than the quarter note. Two eighth notes can fit into one quarter note. Eighth notes are often paired together to complete the beat. When this occurs, the eighth notes are typically beamed together at the end of their stems. If there are multiple eighth notes consecutively, they can all be beamed together.

Because eighth notes are a division of the beat, it is best to approach them by counting with divisions of the beat. For example "1-and" would be two eighth notes on beat one of a measure. When timing out eighth notes, the two sounds should occur within the same beat. Some methods use the word "run-ning" to represent the two sounds of the eighth notes moving faster. In the example below, there are two measures filled with eighth notes. Their various beam appearances are included with counts on the bottom.

To assist with learning new songs and developing a feeling for the timing, it is encouraged to listen to the music you are studying. The tunes or melodies included in this guide are all commonly heard and easily searchable by title on any music streaming service.

Whole note, half note, quarter note, and eighth note are all durations of sound. Music also features durations of silence, and in sheet music, these correspond directly with the notes studied above. Classified as **rests**, these silent durations share the same names with the durations of sound.

Rest Image	Name	Duration
	Whole rest	A full measure, most commonly 4 counts
	Half rest	2 counts
	Quarter rest	1 count
	Eighth rest	½ count

Meter, Measures, and Bar Lines

Music is structured using several musical symbols and markings that make it more cohesive and organized for the performer to read and interpret. The structural markings are like punctuation, and will always be found in properly notated music. These three main elements of musical structure are **meter**, **measures**, and **bar lines**.

In music, meter is the grouping of beats into measures. Meter is not necessarily heard, but it is always felt, like the musical pulse we discussed earlier. The meter of music can vary in regard to how many beats are grouped together. The most common groupings of beats are two's, three's, and four's.

All music is structured and organized into measures, and these measures are divided by bar lines. Bar lines are the short vertical lines that organize the music in respect to the meter. These bar lines group a specified number of beats together that remains consistent for each measure.

At the beginning of any piece of music will be two numbers stacked on top of each other (like a fraction). The top number indicates how many beats are in each measure. The most common **time signature** in music is 4/4. In this time signature, there will be four beats per measure. The bottom number indicates what type of note gets the beat. To begin with, you will only see a four on the bottom, which indicates that the quarter note receives the beat. The time signature notates the meter, and these terms are, on a basic level, interchangeable.

It is common practice to count the duration of notes in relation to the time signature. For example, a whole note (four count note) would count "1-2-3-4" and take the whole measure as one long sound. Two half notes (two count notes) would divide that into two sounds in a measure, as "1-2 3-4", with a separation between beats 2 and 3. A measure of four quarter notes (one count notes) would count "1-2-3-4" with a quarter note occurring on each beat.

In the example below, notice the time signature located next to the treble clef. Each measure in this example contains a total of four beats. The bar lines organize the music into six measures all together. At the end of the line is a special type of bar line, called a **double bar line**. The double bar line indicates the end of the music. Whole notes, half notes, and quarter notes are featured in this example with their respective counts below each measure.

Additional time signatures that you may see in music for beginners will be 3/4 and 2/4. 3/4 indicates that there are three beats per measure, and 2/4 indicates that there are two beats per measure.

In order to properly train timing and rhythm, many instructors and students use an apparatus called a metronome. A metronome is a tool that produces an audible sound, such as a click or beep, and ideally a synchronized visual motion component, like a pendulum or a blinking light. Tapping or clapping with the metronome will train the ears and body to hear and feel a steady pulse. They are available in multiple formats such as physical devices (purchasable online and at local music retailers), interactive online metronomes, and even as applications for smartphones.

Pick-Up Notes

At the beginning of many musical pieces, you may find an incomplete measure. This can be various types of notes in regard to duration, and what makes it unique is that the measure is not complete. For example, a 3/4 time signature stipulates that there are three beats per measure, but there are special instances where there may be a single beat at the very opening of a musical selection. This is called **pick-up notes**, or **anacrusis**.

In the example above, the single quarter note is an anacrusis or pick-up note. In this case, the quarter note occurs on beat three. It is as if there are rests preceding the quarter note, but they are unwritten since it is the beginning of the music. It is best to count the beats that would lead up to the pick-up note when preparing to play.

When music contains an anacrusis measure, the final measure of the piece should compensate for that if properly notated. Notice that in the example above, the final measure is two beats. Together, the first and final measure are worth a total of three beats, which matches the time signature.

Pick-up notes can feature multiple notes and can be found in various time signatures. When determining how to count any anacrusis, fill in the beats before the notes with imaginary rests that would complete the measure in relation to the time signature. This will help determine what beat or beats of the measure the pick-up note occurs on to help the player count into the song correctly.

Rhythmic Dots and Ties

There are two markings used in music to add duration to notes. The first to discuss is the **tie**. A tie is a curved line that connects two notes of the same pitch level (frequency).

The tie functions to take the two durations values, and combine them into one longer duration. For example, a whole note is four counts, and could be tied to a quarter note, which is one count (the first measure below). Rather than having two separate sounds, the tie would create one note that lasts for five counts. Ties are commonly used to create durations longer than four, or to create durations that cross over bar lines.

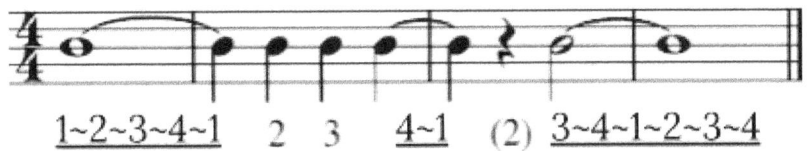

A second marking is the **rhythmic dot**. This dot functions to give us durations that are between half notes, quarter notes, and eighth notes. For example, up to this point in the guide we have not seen a note that represents a duration of three counts. While it would be possible to tie together a half note (2 counts) and a quarter note (1 count) to create a 3 count duration of sound, this is not proper notation. Rather than using ties to achieve a three count duration, we use the rhythmic dot. To create the three count duration, a dot is added after a half note, and changed into what we call the dotted half note (see the first measure below).

Let's further examine the function of the rhythmic dot. In the example of a half note, the dot added one beat to the value of the original duration (half note=2 counts). However, the duration the dot adds is dependent upon the note it is attached. The rhythmic dot adds half of the value of whatever note to which it is attached. So, if it were added to a quarter note, which is one count, the dot would be valued at ½ of a count, and a dotted quarter would be counted for 1 ½ beats total.

Dotted quarter notes and dotted half notes are the most commonly used dotted rhythms, and will get you through this guide, preliminary music, and most beginner level music. We will focus on the application of these two dotted rhythms.

Additional Tempo Markings

Tempo markings expand beyond beats per minute numbers for metronomes. Italian terms are frequently used to describe the speed of the music. These terms are more descriptive, and can also imply mood and expression. The following table contains a few of the most commonly seen tempo markings seen in music. There are metronome indicators included for a general ballpark of what each term implies in context of speed.

Common Tempo Markings

Largo	40-60 BPM
Adagio	66-76 BPM
Andante	76-108 BPM
Moderato	98-112 BPM
Allegro	120-156 BPM
Presto	168-200 BPM

Other Symbols and Markings

Music contains a vast amount of markings and terminology. This guide contains the most essential and widely used to assist any beginning recorder player as they start their journey on the instrument. To continue gaining knowledge of terminology, symbols, and markings, acquiring a musical dictionary may be of interest. For now, here are additional markings you may encounter in your first recorder pieces.

 This "C" symbol represents **common time**. Common time refers to 4/4 because it is the most common time signature used in music.

 A *fermata* is a symbol written above or below a note or chord that indicates for that note or chord to be sustained for longer than its usual duration. The duration is unspecified and is in the hands of the conductor or performer to interpret how long is appropriate to the musical line. The image of the symbol is pictured to the left.

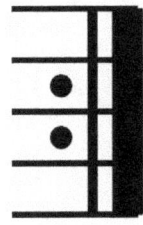 When accompanied by two dots, the double bar line takes on a new meaning. Rather than indicating the end of a musical selection, the dots signify to repeat the music. This can be a line, multiple lines, or an entire song. It depends if the **repeat sign** is paired with additional repeat signs or other markings. Most commonly in beginner level music, it will be found at the end of a line or section and indicate to repeat back to the beginning of the musical selection.

While slightly beyond beginning level, **phrasing** is an important concept to mention. Phrasing refers to how musical lines are grouped together and separated, determined by the melodic structure. Put simply, phrases are musical sentences. Our ears can perceive their beginnings and ends when heard and performed correctly in regards to how the phrase is structured. While this may be difficult the discern as a beginner, there is a marking that can be used to guide the phrasing of a musical piece.

❜ Because the recorder requires air to create music, composers and editors may use **breath marks** to indicate where the phrases of the music end. A breath mark looks like a small apostrophe and is located above and between notes on the staff. Breathing at the breath mark helps to interpret how the composer intended the phrasing to be performed.

Recorders Tuned in "C"

Recorders tuned in "C" to study are the soprano and tenor recorders. Being tuned in "C" means that when all of the tone holes are covered, the note produced is a "C". The difference between the soprano and tenor recorder is in its size and sounding octave. An octave is the distance of eight notes. Simply put, the tenor recorder sounds lower and the soprano recorder sounds higher, and they play the same letter names when covering the same tone holes.

When attempting the following notes, be sure that the required tone holes are completely covered by the corresponding finger tips. If there are any leaks from the fingers not sealing the tone holes, the proper sounds will not be produced.

If you are playing on an alto or bass recorder, you may skip to page 43 from here to learn the specifics of your instrument. You are welcome to still read about recorders tuned in "C" because most of the knowledge is transferable. All of the following concepts will be applied to the alto and bass recorders in the portion about recorders tuned in "F".

Notes B-A-G

As we discussed previously, letter names are used to organize and identify notes in music. The musical alphabet contains seven letters, so the standard lettering system for musical notes is A-B-C-D-E-F-G. In this portion, we will begin learning how to create these notes on any recorder tuned in "C", such as the soprano or tenor recorders.

To begin, establish proper posture and hand position. Next, cover tone holes 0 and 1 with the correct fingers (left hand thumb and index finger). Create the desired sound by starting with the "du" articulation technique previously discussed, and blowing a gentle, steady air stream into the recorder. This finger combination will produce the note "B".

In recorder music, this "B" note would be placed on the centerline of the staff, line 3. The "B" note that we are sounding with the recorder is pictured below as a few types of notes on that line.

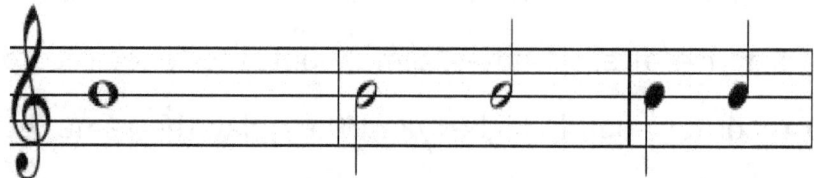

In the image above, each note has a note head that is centered on the middle line of staff. The first note on the far left is a whole note, and it directs the "B" note to be played and sustained for four beats. This means that you would blow steadily for four continuous counts before stopping the note. The second note is a half note, and signifies to sustain the note for two counts. The third note is a quarter note, which is a one count note. Notes of any duration (whole=4, half=2, quarter=1) found on this center line will use the "B" fingering to produce the correct note. For a note on this line, the stem can face either direction. Feel free to try your "B" note with the above durations.

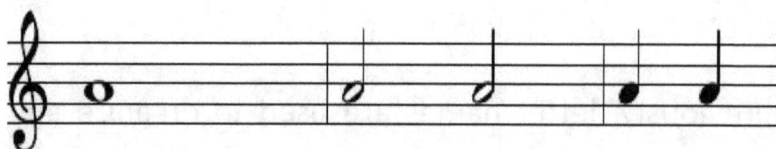

The next note to try is "A". To play "A", we are going to keep the "B" fingers and add finger number two. This means tone holes 0, 1, and 2 are all completely covered to produce this note. "A" should sound slightly lower than "B" did. On the treble clef staff, this "A" is notated on the space right below "B". In the image above, this "A" is notated on the treble clef staff as a whole note, half note, and quarter note. This note is on the second space from the bottom of the staff. The stem will face up for this note because it is below the middle line of the staff. Try playing the "A" notes above on your recorder.

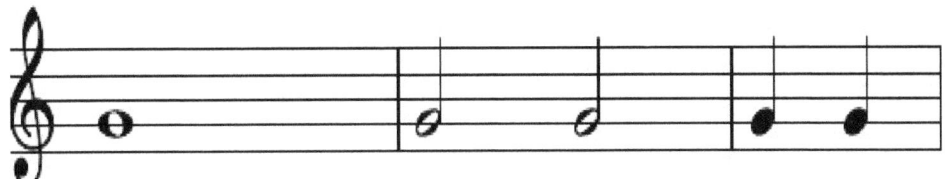

By adding the final finger of the left hand to tone hole 3, we have our third note, "G". This note is one step below "A" in sound, and is written on the line directly below our "A" note. To produce the note "G", tone holes 0, 1, 2, and 3 should all be covered. This "G" is pictured on the treble clef staff above on the second line from the bottom of the staff. Try playing these "G" notes on your recorder.

Remember to begin each note with a "du" tongue to start the sound. Once the fingers have gained accuracy between the notes, try playing them in the sequences below to gain proficiency with changing notes. At first, go slowly, then increase the speed for a challenge. Tone holes 0 and 1 will remain closed at all times because "B", "A", and "G" all require them to be covered. Be sure to use a "du" tongue to begin each note.

B-B-A-A-G-G-A-A-B-B   B-A-G-A-B-A-G   B-A-B-A-B-A-B-A   B-G-B-G-B-G-B-G

Now, let's play our first song, Hot Cross Buns. This song uses the three notes "B", "A", and "G". There are two versions of Hot Cross Buns below. The first is notated in letter names occurring from left to right. The dashes indicate to sustain the note, or to blow air for a longer note. The second version is in standard music notation with music notes on the staff.

Hot Cross Buns

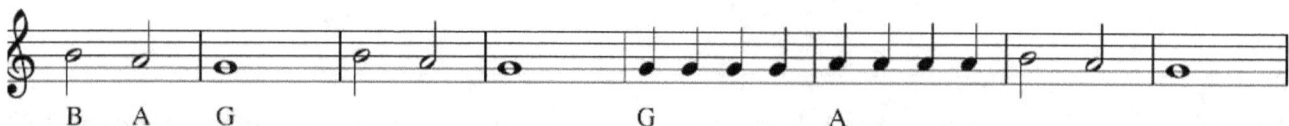

For now, use whichever version is easiest for you to read. The focus currently is making sound with your recorder. Music reading proficiency will continue to develop with practice. If you have never heard the tune, listen to Hot Cross Buns to gain familiarity with the timing and sounds. When practicing any music, regularly check that you are maintaining good posture and hand position.

Reading a Fingering Diagram

Now that you've rehearsed your first song, we can continue learning additional notes. As we continue to explore new notes, it may take more than one day to memorize all of the fingerings for the various notes. Luckily, it is standard to have a fingering chart at hand for reference of proper finger combinations for all notes on the recorder. The fingerings featured in this part of our guide are for soprano and tenor recorders, which are both in recorders tuned in "C". All of the fingerings and notes within practical range on the recorder are included at the end of this guide. There is a complete fingering chart for both recorders in "C" and recorders in "F". When using the charts as reference, make certain you are viewing the correct chart for your instrument.

To the left is a standard, blank, finger diagram. It is oriented as if viewing the recorder from the front. The circle to the side represents the tone hole on the back of the recorder. The blank circles represent open tone holes. To the right, the holes are all colored to represent the tone holes being covered. Darkened circles represent closed tone holes. In the image to the left, all tone holes would be open with no fingers. In the image to the right, all tone holes would be covered. (Note: there are fingering diagrams and charts that list the thumb tone hole at the top of the diagram. When viewing a fingering chart, be certain to read the headings and layout carefully. The fingering diagrams in this guide will be formatted with the back tone hole to the side, like the diagrams below

Let's examine the fingering diagrams for the notes we've learned so far – B, A, and G. Below are the fingering diagrams for each of these notes. Included with the finger diagrams are the letter name and an image of the note on the treble clef staff.

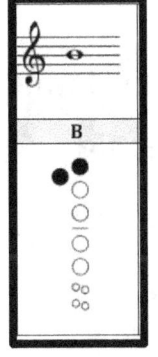 First is the fingering for B. Tone holes 0 and 1 are closed.

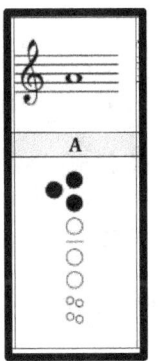 Next is the fingering for A. Tone holes 0, 1, 2 are closed.

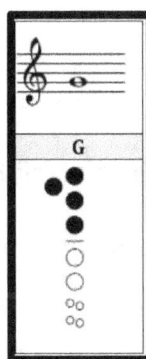 This is the fingering for G. Tone holes 0, 1, 2, 3 are closed.

When reading a finger chart, it is typically presumed that the player understands which fingers to use to cover the tone holes indicated by the darkened circles. Every time you pick up your recorder to practice, always ensure that your hands and fingers are placed properly.

The ability to read a finger chart will continue to prove useful as we learn additional notes. Let's continue with two more notes for the left hand, "C" and "D".

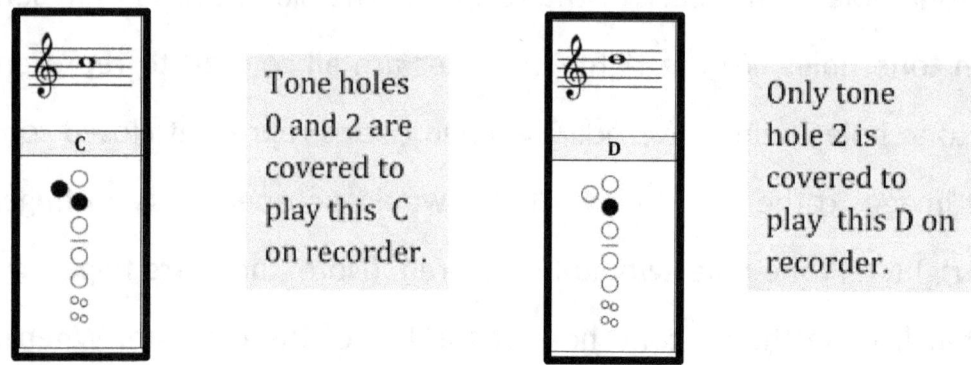

This "C" is higher in pitch than "B", and this "D" is even higher than the "C". "D" is the first note we've studied so far that requires tone hole zero to be open. When lifting your left thumb from tone hole 0, it is best to either roll it downward and away from the tone hole or to lift it and keep it close to the tone hole when not covering it. Keeping all fingers close to their assigned tone holes is great technique for all of your fingers. Minimal distance between the fingers and their respective tone holes makes it easier to transition between notes.

Here are the notes we've learned so far notated on the treble clef staff, listed lowest to highest from left to right as whole notes (four counts). Try playing these notes up and down to gain fluency in changing your fingers between notes. Fingers should be slightly curved and remain close to tone holes when not covering them.

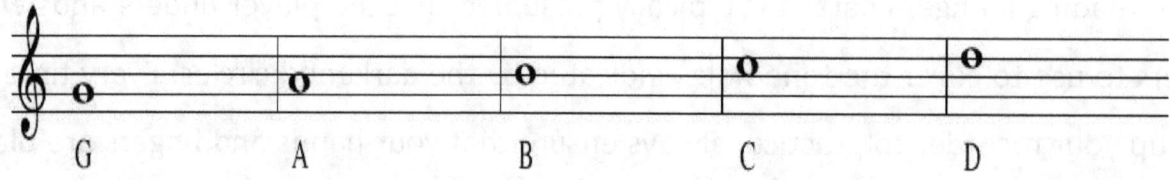

Let's use all five notes in a melody by the late, great composer, Ludwig Van Beethoven. This time, the sheet music is included with the letter names of the notes on the first line labeled to help you get started. Initially, play new music very slowly to allow yourself time to think and coordinate your body. Remember when playing to use a "du" tongue to begin each note. It may also be helpful to listen to a recording of the song to gain familiarity.

Ode to Joy

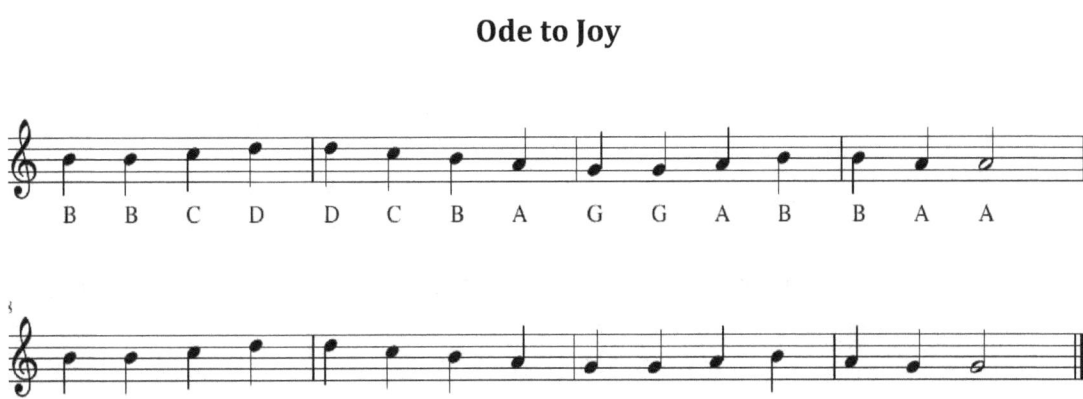

The notes we've learned so far have been combinations of the fingers of the left hand. As we add fingers and cover tone holes with the fingers of the right hand, the notes will continue to sound lower in pitch than G.

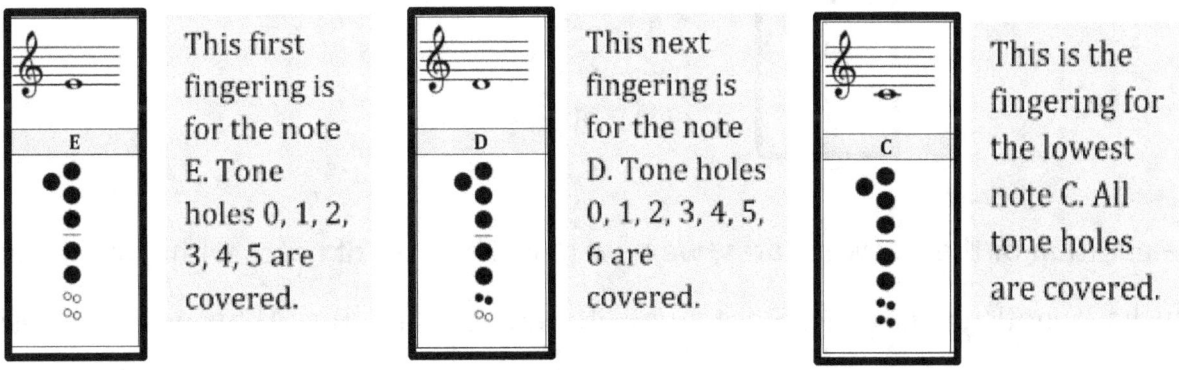

This first fingering is for the note E. Tone holes 0, 1, 2, 3, 4, 5 are covered.

This next fingering is for the note D. Tone holes 0, 1, 2, 3, 4, 5, 6 are covered.

This is the fingering for the lowest note C. All tone holes are covered.

These lower notes require a gentle air stream to produce the correct pitch. The "C" is the lowest note possible on any recorder tuned in "C" like the soprano and tenor recorders. Notice that when playing "C" or "D", both of the double holes for tone hole 6 and 7 are covered.

Try playing this song that incorporates one of our newest notes, "E". It also features a new symbol at the end of the line, called a repeat sign. This repeat sign indicates to play the line again, for a total of two times.

Rain, Rain, Go Away

The final note to study in this portion was saved for last because of its unique fingering. In between "E" and "G" in letter steps is "F". It is the first forked fingering we've encountered. The phrase forked fingering is used to describe a fingering that has an open hole followed by closed holes below it.

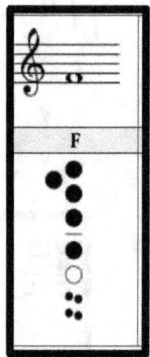

To play F, cover tone holes 0, 1, 2, 3, 4, 6, and 7. The only open tone hole is 5.

With the addition of these lower notes, we now have a full set of notes within an octave. You may have noticed that there are two different C's and D's. The ones with less fingers create higher pitches, while the C and D that cover more holes create lower pitches. They are often referred to as high C and D and low C and D respectively. A more specific classification is referring to the lowest C and D as being in the first octave, and the next C and D would belong to the second octave.

Because notes ascend and descend in the same sequence as the first seven letters of the alphabet, eight notes apart will be the same letter. For example, if we list the notes we've learned on recorder starting and ending on C (omitting high D for now), there are eight total letters. Notes that are the same letter name and eight steps apart are considered to be an octave apart.

        C   D   E   F   G   A   B   C

        1   2   3   4   5   6   7   8

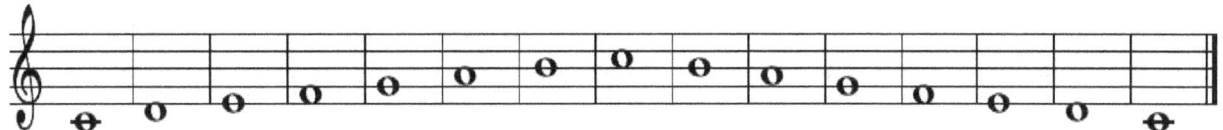

When we play eight notes in a stepwise sequence such as above, this is called a **scale**. Scales are a great way to train your eyes, fingers, and ears to play notes accurately. The specific scale above is the C scale, named appropriately because it begins and ends on C.

Practice the following C scale exercise to gain proficiency in the notes studied in this chapter.

Sharps and Flats

Before beginning to study the notes higher than the high "D" from the last chapter, we must first analyze the notes between the letter names discussed. Earlier in this guide, we briefly discussed sharp, flat, and natural signs. To review, there are half steps and whole steps possible between two consecutive notes. To best visualize this concept, we are going to use the piano keyboard.

The white keys labeled above are the eight notes of the "C" scale. In between most of these white keys are black keys. When two keys are directly beside each other, they are a half step apart. They are also referred to as semitones. In this chapter, we are going to examine those in-between notes and their fingerings.

First, let's establish how these notes are labeled. To classify these half steps or semitones, two symbols are used: the sharp sign and the flat sign.

A sharp sign (♯) looks similar to a pound sign or hashtag. It is used to indicate that a note is to be raised a half step. That means that the note between "C" and "D" could be called a "C sharp" (C♯), because it is a half-step above "C". This note would require a new fingering and have a sound that is halfway in pitch between "C" and "D".

A flat sign looks like a lowercase "b". It is used to indicate that a note is to be lowered by a half step. This means that the note between "C" and "D" could also be called "D flat" (D♭). It would be the same fingering and sound as "C♯". This means that our "in-between" notes, or semitones, can have more than one name for the same note or fingering. Both "C sharp" and "D flat" are considered enharmonic equivalents. Whether the note will appear as a flat or sharp in music varies, so it is best to be familiar with both enharmonic names and notations. In this guide, both names and notations will be displayed with the fingering diagram.

Let's begin with "C sharp/D flat" (C♯/D♭). Specifically, we are examining this note in the second octave. To play the second octave "C♯/D♭", a new fingering combination is used.

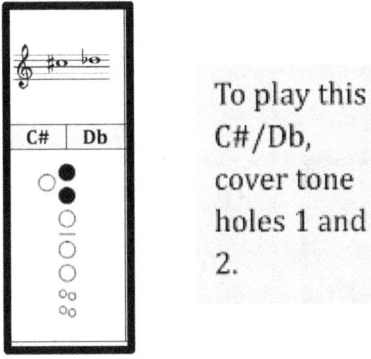

To play this C#/Db, cover tone holes 1 and 2.

Some letter names do not have a half step between them because they are naturally a half step apart. There is no half step between "B" and "C" or "E" and "F". Below is a chart of all of the enharmonic equivalents in letter names. The fingering chart at the end of this guide lists the fingerings along with both the sharp and flat name for each note.

C# = Db
D# = Eb
E# = F
Fb = E
F# = Gb
G# = Ab
A# = Bb
B# = C
Cb = B

Above the second octave "D" is "D♯/E♭" of the second octave (higher notes) This note is a half-step higher than "D".

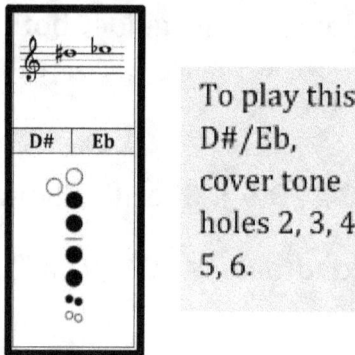

To play this D#/Eb, cover tone holes 2, 3, 4, 5, 6.

Let's learn the fingers of more sharp and flat notes in the first octave (lower notes). Between "A" and "B" is "A sharp/B flat", or "A#/B♭".

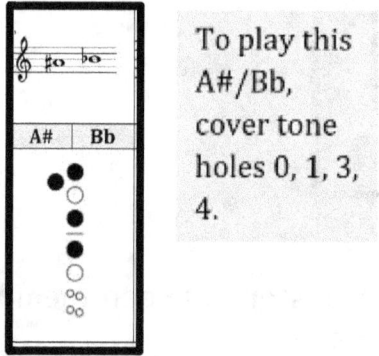

To play this A#/Bb, cover tone holes 0, 1, 3, 4.

Between "F" and "G" in sound and on the staff is "F#/G♭".

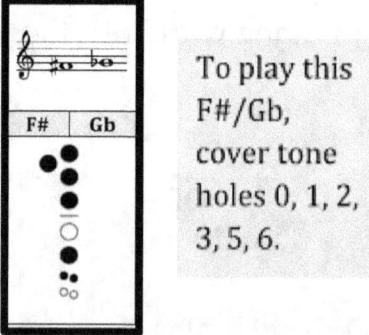

To play this F#/Gb, cover tone holes 0, 1, 2, 3, 5, 6.

These next fingerings involve new alterations to tone hole 6 and 7, the double tone holes near the end of the recorder. To create the half steps or semitones between the first octave G/A, D/E, and C/D, a single one of the double tone holes will be covered on either tone hole 6 or 7. This is referred to as half covering a tone hole, since tone holes 6 and 7 are considered to be the entirety of both of the little holes. When viewing and applying the fingering for each of these notes, the single, tiny tone hole to be covered will be closest to finger 6 or 7. When writing the fingering out with numbers, the 6 or 7 is commonly written with a line through it to indicate half of the tone hole being covered.

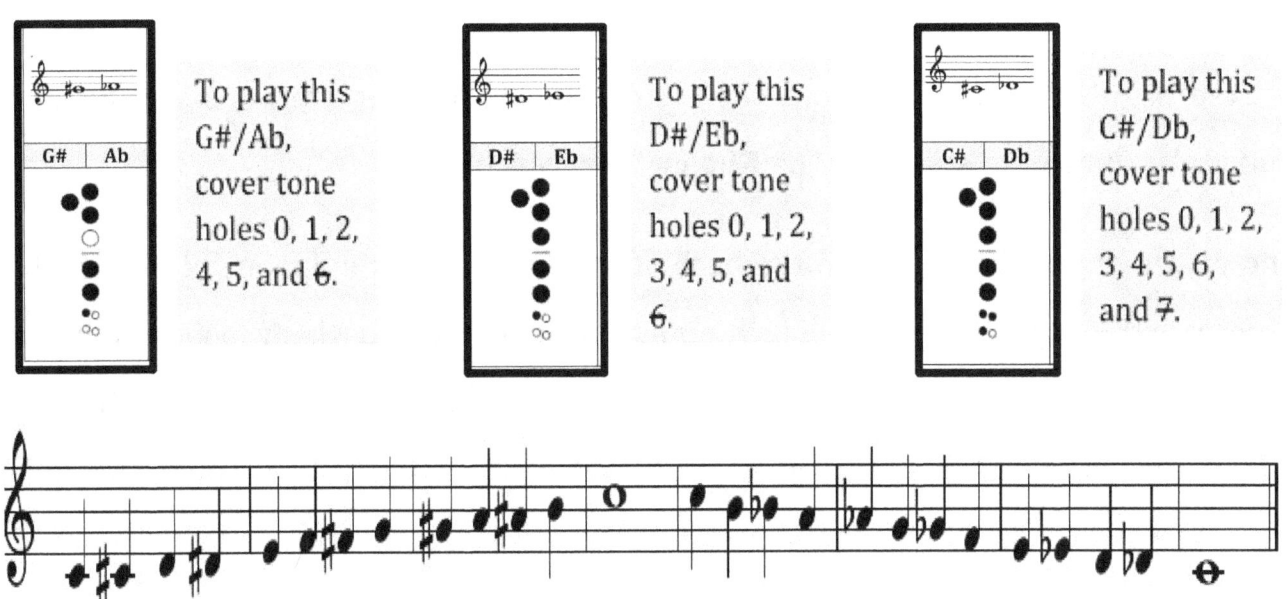

The line of music below is the C **Chromatic** Scale. The word chromatic refers to how the notes are ascending and descending by half steps within an octave, which in this example, is from our low (first octave) "C" to high (second octave) "C". The ascending part of the scale uses the sharp note names, while the descending part of the scale uses the flat note names.

Advanced Techniques

Notes beyond the second octave "D♯/E♭" we studied earlier require special techniques and fingerings. When initially learning the fingers and sounds of these notes, they may not sound particularly pleasant. Techniques for improving the tone of your notes will be discussed in the next section. The development of a beautiful tone on any instrument occurs over time and practice. Let's first get the fingerings established.

For any note above the second octave "D♯/E♭", the thumb hole on the back of the recorder is only partially covered rather than completely closed. This is represented in a fingering diagram with the bottom half of tone hole 0 being shaded. The half-shaded circle indicates for the left thumb to "leak" air from this tone hole by rolling the thumb back to slightly open the tone hole. The thumb should not completely uncover the hole. This is also known as "**shading**", "**half-holing**", or "**pinching**".

The placement of the thumb on the back of the recorder will influence how smoothly notes will transition to these new high notes. Engaging the knuckle of the left thumb in order to be able to roll it on and off the tone hole allows for a fluent motion. The term "thumb pinching" is used to represent the ideal way to partially cover the hole. Experiment with placing your thumb so that you can pivot the thumb to roll to cover and leak the tone hole.

The exact size of the thumb opening can vary on individual recorders and is determined by listening to the clarity and tone of the sound. High notes speak easily when the opening is smaller. However, if the opening is too small, the tone quality will suffer, and the opening may need to be increased. It may take some experimentation to achieve the best ratio of open versus closed. High notes also require a firm tongue followed by a stronger, faster air stream.

To begin applying this "leaking" technique with the left thumb, let's begin with the second octave "E", "G", and "A". These notes have been chosen first because their fingerings will be more familiar. For each of these notes, the fingers on the front of the recorder remain the same as the first octave. The alteration is entirely in the leaking of the thumb hole on the back.

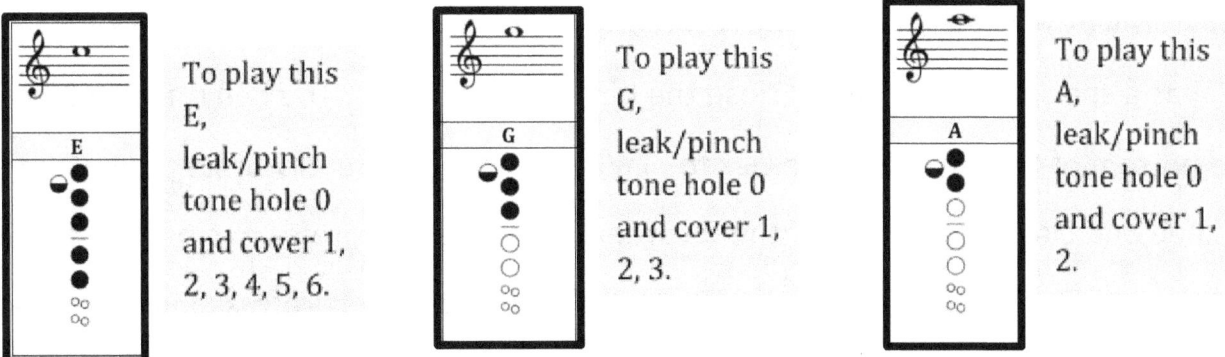

Practicing the following musical exercise will help in approaching these new notes. Practice transitioning from the lower note to the higher note versions of "E", "G", and "A" by leaking the thumb hole when changing to the higher note. Begin slowly and use a "du" tongue to start each note. Remember to use faster air when executing the second octave notes.

The remaining high notes of the second octave that utilize the "thumb pinching" technique all have unique and challenging fingerings. The notes we have examined so far will allow you to begin playing music at a level appropriate for a beginner to early intermediate level player on recorder. As you progress in your playing, more advanced music will become accessible, and you will come across some of these notes.

The highest three notes on the recorder are the third octave "C", "C♯/D♭", and "D". They are quite advanced and the highest in sound. The third octave notes are reserved for advanced recorder music. As you can see in the fingering chart at the back of the guide, these have challenging fingerings. They will be the most difficult notes to sound for most players.

When viewing the fingering chart for recorders in "C", notice that the third octave "C♯/D♭" has a special instruction to "close the bell with the knee". The bell is the opening at the bottom of the recorder. In order to play this note, you literally press the bell into your knee and close off the end of the recorder. Some methods refer to closing the bell as "closing hole 8", since it is beyond tone hole 7. There are professional recorders constructed with a mechanism that closes this hole as well. Unless your recorder has this mechanism, you will need to cover the hole using your thigh/knee to play the third octave "C♯/D♭". When standing, this is achieved by slightly lifting the leg and bringing the torso into your upper thigh where they meet. When sitting, the same is done with lifting the knee and bending the torso toward each other, but the end of the recorder will meet the leg closer to the knee.

Recorders Tuned in "F"

When recorders are said to be "tuned in F" it means that when all of the tone holes are covered, the sounding note is "F". So while there are fingering combinations in common between recorders tuned in "C" and recorders tuned in "F", all of the letter names are changed. The sopranino, alto, and bass recorders are popular recorder choices that are tuned in "F".

To begin, establish proper posture and hand position. Next, cover tone holes 0 and 1 with the correct fingers (left hand thumb and index finger). Create the desired sound by starting with the "du" articulation technique previously discussed, and blowing a gentle, steady air stream into the recorder. This finger combination will produce the note "E".

In recorder music, this "E" note would be placed on the top space of the staff, or the fourth space from the bottom. The "E" note that we are sounding with the recorder is pictured below as a few types of notes on that line.

In the image above, each note has a note head that sits on space 4, the top space between the lines of the staff. The first note on the far left is a whole note, and it directs the "E" note to be played and sustained for four beats. This means that you would blow steadily for four continuous counts before stopping the note. The second note is a half note, and signifies to sustain the note for two counts. The third note is a quarter note, which is a one count note. Notes of any duration (whole=4, half=2, quarter=1) found on this top line will use the "E" fingering to produce the correct note. For a note with a stem on this space, the stem will face down because it is above the centerline of the staff. Feel free to try your "E" note with the above durations.

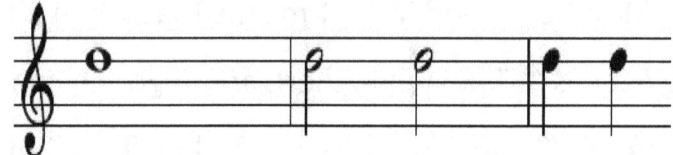

The next note to try is "D". To play "D", we are going to keep the "E" fingers and add finger number two. This means tone holes 0, 1, and 2 are all completely covered to produce this note. "D" should sound slightly lower than "E" did. On the treble clef staff, this "D" is notated on the line right below "E", which is line 4 when counting from the bottom of the staff. In the image above, this "D" is notated on the treble clef staff as a whole note, half note, and quarter note. Try playing the "D" notes above on your recorder.

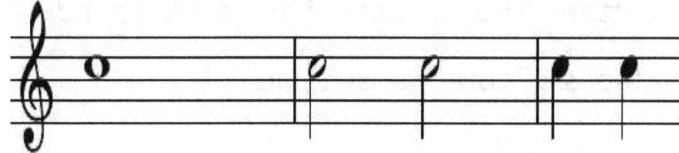

By adding the final finger of the left hand to tone hole 3, we have our third note, "C". This note is one step below "D" in sound, and is written on the space directly below our "D" note. To produce the note "C", tone holes 0, 1, 2, and 3 should all be covered. This "C" is pictured on the treble clef staff above on space 3. Try playing this "C" on your recorder.

Let's put these three notes together into a classic folk song, "Hot Cross Buns". Featured below are a letter diagram of the notes followed by the songs notated on the staff. For both, read the notes or letter names from left to right. The dashes represent the longer durations of the half notes (two counts) and whole notes (four counts) in the music. Remember to set your posture and ensure the correct hand position before beginning. Use a "du" tongue to begin each note.

Hot Cross Buns

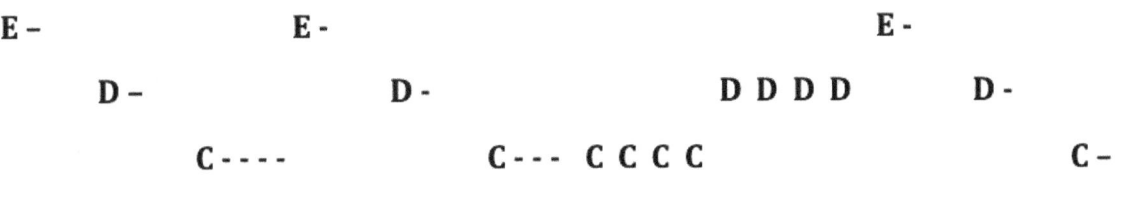

Reading a Fingering Diagram

As we continue to explore new notes, it may take more than one day to memorize all of the fingerings for the various notes. Luckily, it is standard to have a fingering chart at hand for reference of proper finger combinations for all notes on the recorder. There are various recorder fingering charts available for free download. Be sure to check if the fingering chart is written for recorders in "C" or "F". The fingerings featured in this part of the guide are for alto and bass recorders, which are both in "F". There is also a recorder fingering chart included at the end of this guide for both recorders in "C" and in "F".

To the left is a standard, blank, finger chart. It is oriented as if viewing the recorder from the front. The circle to the side represents the tone hole on the back of the recorder. The blank circles represent open tone holes. To the right, the holes are all colored to represent the tone holes being covered. Darkened circles represent closed tone holes. In the image to the left, all tone holes would be open with no fingers. In the image to the right, all tone holes would be covered. (Note: there are fingering charts that list the thumb tone hole at the top of the diagram. When choosing a fingering chart, be certain to read the headings and layout carefully and choose one that is easiest for you to read and understand.)

When reading a finger chart or diagram, it is typically presumed that the player understands which fingers to use to cover the tone holes indicated by the darkened circles. Every time you pick up your recorder to practice, always ensure that your hands and fingers are placed properly. Refer to page 11 to review hand position, finger placement, and finger numbers.

Let's apply fingering diagrams to the three notes we just studied, "E", "D", and "C".

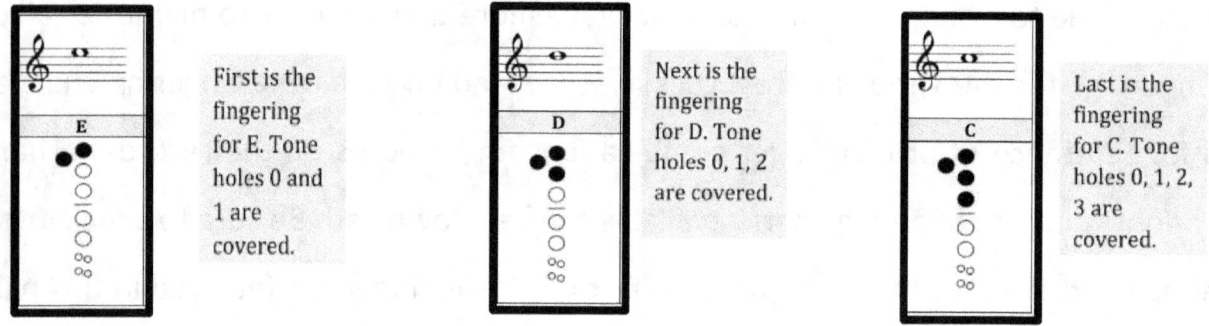

First is the fingering for E. Tone holes 0 and 1 are covered.

Next is the fingering for D. Tone holes 0, 1, 2 are covered.

Last is the fingering for C. Tone holes 0, 1, 2, 3 are covered.

The ability to read a fingering diagram will continue to prove useful as we learn additional notes. Let's continue with two more notes for the left hand, "F" and "G". "G" is the first note to open tone hole 0. This means your left thumb will need to either lift and hover over that tone hole or roll downward to uncover it. This "F" and "G" belong to the second octave of a recorder in "F".

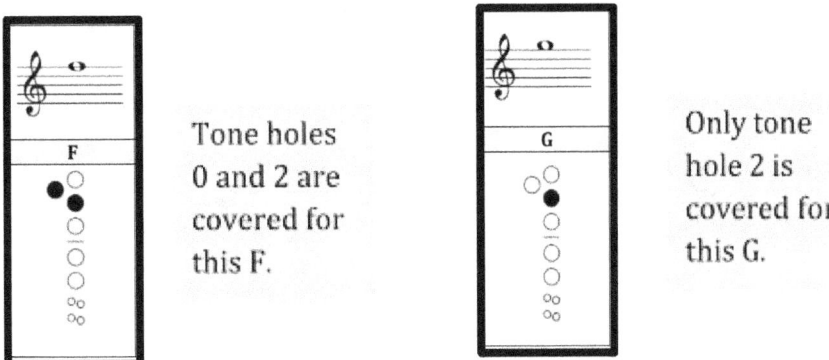

This "F" is higher in pitch than "E", and this "G" is even higher than "F". Here are the notes we've learned so far (in this portion of the guide) notated on the treble clef staff, listed lowest to highest from left to right as whole notes (four counts). Try playing these notes up and down to gain fluency in changing your fingers between notes. Your fingers should be slightly curved and hover close to the tone holes when uncovered.

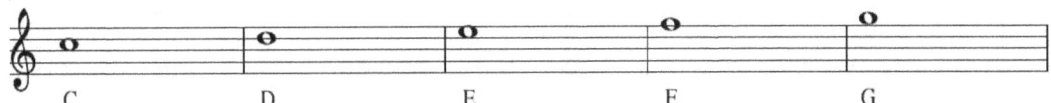

With these five notes, you can play a melody by the late, great composer, Ludwig Van Beethoven. This time, the sheet music is included with the letters in the first line labeled to help you get started. Initially, play new music very slowly to allow yourself time to think and coordinate your fingers, tongue, and air. Remember when playing to use a "du" tongue to begin each note.

Ode to Joy

The notes we've learned so far have been combinations of the fingers of the left hand. As we add fingers and cover tone holes with the fingers of the right hand, the notes will continue to sound lower in pitch than C.

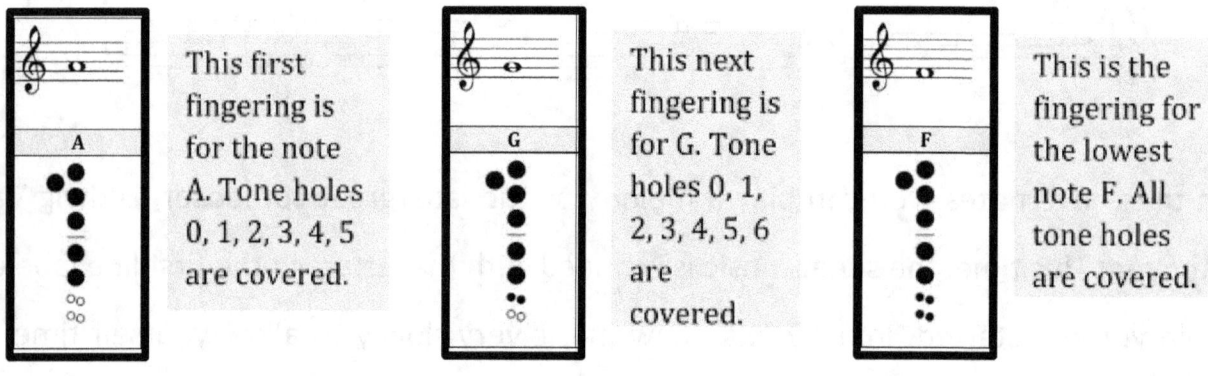

This first fingering is for the note A. Tone holes 0, 1, 2, 3, 4, 5 are covered.

This next fingering is for G. Tone holes 0, 1, 2, 3, 4, 5, 6 are covered.

This is the fingering for the lowest note F. All tone holes are covered.

These lower notes require a gentle air stream to produce the correct pitch. This "F" is the lowest note possible on any recorder tuned in "F". Notice that when playing "F" or "G", both of the double holes for tone hole 6 and 7 are covered.

Try playing this song that incorporates one of our newest notes, "A".

Rain, Rain, Go Away

The final note to study in this portion was saved for last because of its unique fingering. In between "A" and "C" the sound of pitch is "B". It is the first forked fingering we've encountered in this portion of the guide. The phrase forked fingering is used to describe a fingering that has an open hole followed by closed holes below it.

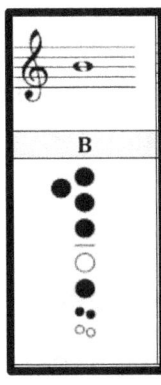

To play B, cover tone holes 0, 1, 2, 3, 4, 6, and 7. The only open tone hole should be 5.

With the addition of these lower notes, we now have a full set of notes within an octave. You may have noticed that there are two different F's and G's. The ones with less fingers create higher pitches, while the "F" and "G" that cover more holes create lower pitches. They are often referred to as high "F" and "G" and low "F" and "G" respectively. A more specific classification is referring to the lowest "F" and "G" as being in the first octave, and the next "F" and "G" as being in the second octave.

Because notes ascend and descend in the same sequence as the first seven letters of the alphabet, eight notes apart will be the same letter. For example, if we list the notes we've learned on recorders in "F" starting and ending on "F" (omitting high "G" for now), there are eight total letters. Notes that are the same letter name and eight steps apart are considered to be an octave apart. In the musical line below, "F" is the first note. If we counted that note as number one, number eighth going up step-by-step would also be "F", but in the next octave.

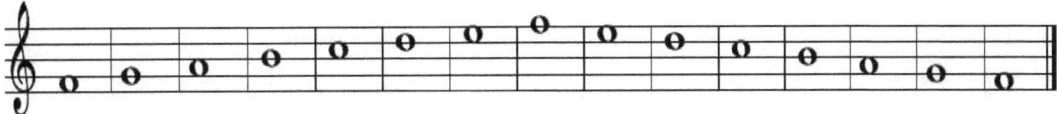

When we play eight notes in a stepwise sequence such as above, this is called a **scale**. Scales are a great way to train your eyes, fingers, and ears to read, play, and hear notes accurately. The specific scale above is a form of an "F" scale (F Lydian scale for you theory buffs), named appropriately because it begins and ends on "F". The more practical and commonly used "F" scale requires an alteration to one of the notes. These alterations come in the form of flats and sharps that will be studied in the next section.

Sharps and Flats

Before beginning to study the notes higher than the high "G" from the last chapter, we must first analyze the notes between the letter names discussed. Earlier in this guide, we briefly discussed sharp, flat, and natural signs. To review, there are half steps and whole steps possible between two consecutive notes. To best visualize this concept, we are going to use part of the piano keyboard.

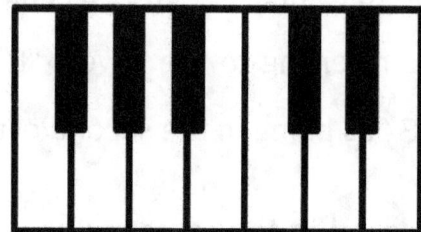

On a piano keyboard, the white keys are the natural notes. These use a letter without any alteration. From left-to-right, or lowest to highest, the white key notes pictured above would be "F-G-A-B-C-D-F". In between most of these white keys are black keys. Two keys directly beside each other, without skipping the any keys, are classified as a half step apart. A half step is also referred to as a semitone. This means there are additional notes between the lettered notes we've learned so far. Let's analyze these half steps.

First, let's establish how these notes are labeled. To classify these half steps or semitones, two symbols are used: the sharp sign and the flat sign.

A sharp sign (♯) looks similar to a pound sign or hashtag. It is used to indicate that a note is to be raised a half step. That means that the note between "F" and "G" could be called a "G sharp" (C♯), because it is a half-step above "G". This note would require a new fingering and have a sound that is halfway in pitch between "F" and "G".

A flat sign looks like a lowercase "b". It is used to indicate that a note is to be lowered by a half step. This means that the note between "F" and "G" could also be called "G flat" (G♭). It would be the same fingering and sound as "F♯". This is because our "in-between" notes, or semitones, can have more than one name for the same note or fingering. Both "F sharp" and "G flat" are considered enharmonic equivalents. Whether the note will appear as a flat or sharp in music varies, so it is best to be familiar with both enharmonic names and notations. In this guide, both names and notations will be displayed with the fingering diagram.

Let's begin with "F sharp/G flat" (F♯/G♭). Specifically, we are examining this note in the second octave. To play the this "F♯/G♭", a new fingering combination is used.

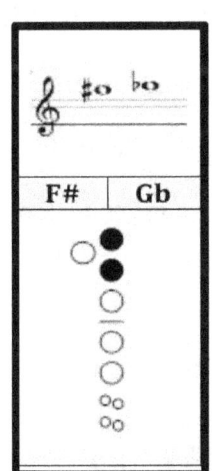

To play this F#/Gb, cover tone holes 1 and 2.

A few letter names do not have a half step between them because they are naturally a half step apart. There is no half step between "B" and "C" or "E" and "F". Below is a chart of all of the enharmonic equivalents in letter names. The fingering chart at the end of this guide lists the fingerings along with both the sharp and flat name for each note.

C# = Db
D# = Eb
E# = F
Fb = E
F# = Gb
G# = Ab
A# = Bb
B# = C
Cb = B

Above the highest note we've played so far, second octave "G", is our second octave "G♯/A♭". This note is a half-step higher than "G".

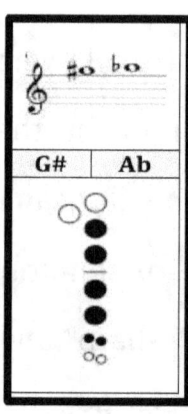

To play this G#/Ab, cover tone holes 2, 3, 4, 5, 6.

Before discussing any additional high notes, let's examine the fingers of more sharp and flat notes in the first octave (lower notes). Between "D" and "E" is "D sharp/E flat", or "D♯/E♭".

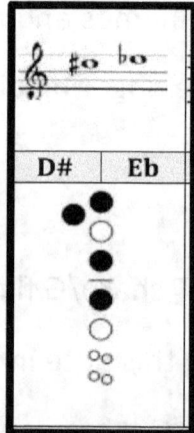

To play this D#/Eb, cover tone holes 0, 1, 3, 4.

Between "A" and "B" in sound and on the staff is "A♯/B♭". This note will frequently be found in music for recorders in "F", such as the alto recorder. This is because scales are built in specific patterns, and the most common form of the "F" scale uses "B♭" rather than "B". If music is in the key of "F", a "B♭" will be either found directly next to the note or in the key signature found at the beginning of the music. For now, the flat sign will be indicated next to the note when it appears.

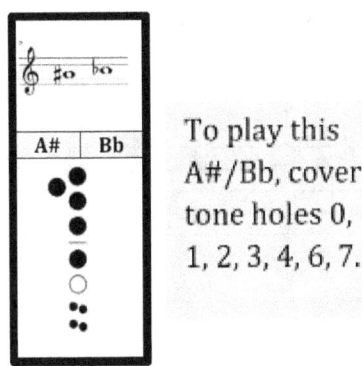

To play this A#/Bb, cover tone holes 0, 1, 2, 3, 4, 6, 7.

These next fingerings involve new alterations to tone hole 6 and 7, the double tone holes near the end of the recorder. To create the half steps or semitones between the first octave G/A, D/E, and C/D, a single one of the double tone holes will be covered on either tone hole 6 or 7. This is referred to as half covering a tone hole, since tone holes 6 and 7 are considered to be the entirety of both of the little holes. When viewing and applying the fingering for each of these notes, the single, tiny tone hole to be covered will be closest to finger 6 or 7. When writing the fingering out with numbers, the 6 or 7 is commonly written with a line through it to indicate half of the tone hole being covered.

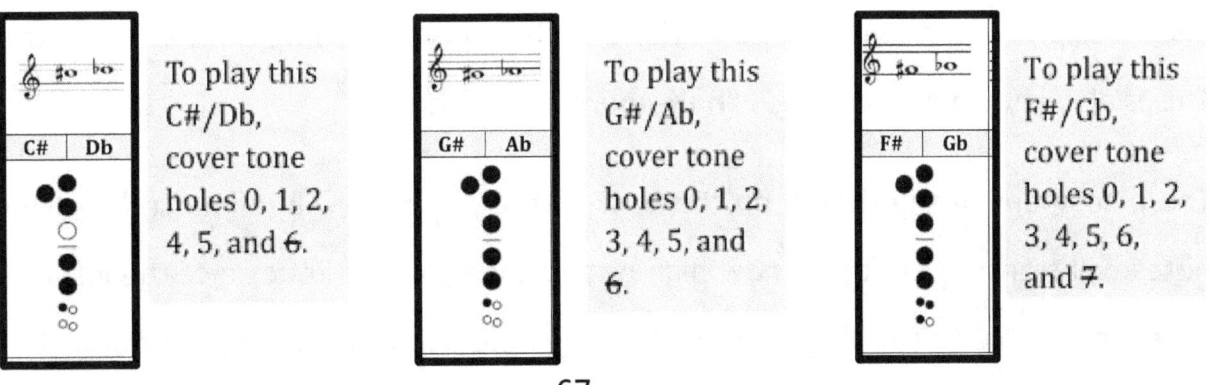

To play this C#/Db, cover tone holes 0, 1, 2, 4, 5, and 6̶.

To play this G#/Ab, cover tone holes 0, 1, 2, 3, 4, 5, and 6̶.

To play this F#/Gb, cover tone holes 0, 1, 2, 3, 4, 5, 6, and 7̶.

To help with the memorization of fingerings and facilitate coordination between notes, it is recommended to practice the chromatic scale. In a chromatic scale, the notes move up and down by half steps, playing every note possible, typically within an octave. The notes in the next musical line are ascending and descending by half steps within an octave, which in the example below is from our low (first octave) "F" to high (second octave) "F". The ascending part of the scale uses the sharp note names, while the descending part of the scale uses the flat note names.

Advanced Techniques

Notes beyond the second octave "G♯/A♭" we studied earlier require special techniques and fingerings. When initially learning the fingers and sounds of these notes, they may not sound particularly pleasant. The development of a beautiful **tone** on any instrument occurs over time and practice. Techniques for improving the tone of your notes will be discussed in the next section. Let's first get the fingerings established.

For any note above the second octave "G♯/A♭", the thumb hole on the back of the recorder is only partially covered rather than completely closed. This is represented in a fingering diagram with the bottom half of tone hole 0 being shaded. The half-shaded circle indicates for the left thumb to "leak" air from this tone hole by rolling the thumb back to slightly open the tone hole. The thumb should not completely uncover the hole. This is also known as **"shading"**, **"half-holing"**, or **"pinching"**.

The placement of the thumb on the back of the recorder will influence how smoothly notes will transition to these new high notes. Engaging the knuckle of the left thumb in order to be able to roll it on and off the tone hole allows for a fluent motion. The term "thumb pinching" is used to represent the ideal way to partially cover the hole. Experiment with placing your thumb so that you can pivot the thumb to roll to cover or leak the tone hole.

The exact size of the thumb opening can vary on individual recorders and is determined by listening to the clarity and tone of the sound. High notes speak easily when the opening is smaller. However, if the opening is too small, the tone quality will suffer, and the opening may need to be increased. It may take some experimentation to achieve the best ratio of open versus closed. High notes also require a firm tongue followed by a stronger, faster air stream.

To begin applying this "leaking" technique with the left thumb, let's begin with the second octave "C", D", and "A". These notes have been chosen first because their fingerings will be more familiar. For each of these notes, the fingers on the front of the recorder remain the same as the first octave. The alteration is entirely in the leaking of the thumb hole on the back.

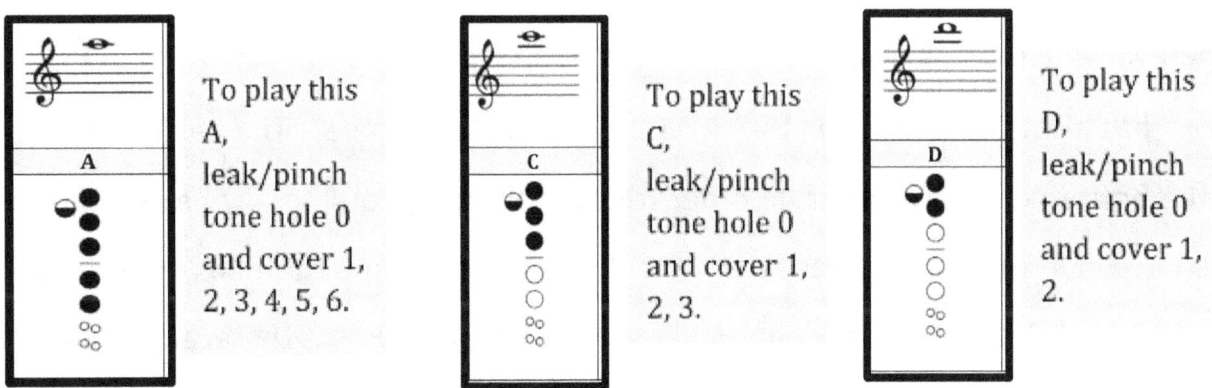

To play this A, leak/pinch tone hole 0 and cover 1, 2, 3, 4, 5, 6.

To play this C, leak/pinch tone hole 0 and cover 1, 2, 3.

To play this D, leak/pinch tone hole 0 and cover 1, 2.

The following musical exercise will help in approaching these new notes. Practice transitioning from the lower note to the higher note versions of "C", "D", and "A" by leaking the thumb hole when changing to the higher note. Begin slowly and use a "du" tongue to start each note. Remember to use faster air when executing the second octave notes.

The remaining high notes of the second octave that utilize the "thumb pinching" technique all have unique and challenging fingerings. The notes we have examined so far will allow you to begin playing music at a level appropriate for a beginner to early intermediate level player on recorder. As you progress in your playing, more advanced music will become accessible, and you will come across some of these notes. Study the fingering chart for the recorder in "F" found at the end of this guide for these fingering diagrams.

The highest three notes on the recorder are the third octave "F", "F♯/G♭", and "G". They are quite advanced and the highest in sound. The third octave notes are reserved for advanced recorder music. As you can see in the fingering chart at the back of the guide, these have challenging fingerings. They will be the most difficult notes to sound for most players.

When viewing the fingering chart for recorders in "F", notice that the third octave "F♯/G♭" has a special instruction to "close the bell with the knee". The bell is the opening at the bottom of the recorder. In order to play this note, you literally have to press the bell into your knee and close the end of the recorder. Some methods refer to closing the bell as "closing hole 8", since it is beyond tone hole 7. There are professional recorders constructed with a mechanism that closes this hole as well. Unless your recorder has this mechanism, you will need to cover the hole using your thigh/knee. When standing, this is achieved by slightly lifting the leg and bringing the torso into your upper thigh where they meet. When sitting, the same is done with lifting the knee and bending the torso toward each other, but the end of the recorder will meet the leg closer to the knee.

Tone Quality and Tuning

On any instrument, the word tone refers to the quality of the sound. Professional instrumentalists and vocalists will have beautiful, refined tone when playing or singing anything they perform. Tone is developed over time and with conscientiousness to how the sound is being produced. When playing either recorders tuned in "F" or "C", the tone quality can be improved with attention to breath control, the formation of the lips, air direction, and air speed. On recorder, this can be challenging and will not occur in a single day or practice session. It will take critical listening skills in order to reflect and react to the sounds you are making, and measuring whether the sound is improving with adjustments over time. The goal is to make daily progress on improving the tone produced through mindful exercises that develop the correct techniques. In this section, we will focus on daily practice techniques and warm-ups that will help improve your tone on the recorder.

Breath Control

One of the keys to learning to control the breath is to practice doing so without the recorder. We did this when learning to make our first sound earlier in the guide. We discussed breathing from the diaphragm and controlling the rate of exhalation. Every practice session should begin with a breathing exercise to remind our body to inhale deeply and exhale gently. Here are a variety of breathing exercises to use before playing. It is only necessary to do one or two of these per practice session.

Breathe in as much as you can, sending the air down low. As you breathe in, feel everything expand around your stomach and sides, keeping everything relaxed. Then, slowly exhale for as long as you can keep the air flowing
Inhale for 4 counts, hold for 4 counts, exhale for 4 counts, and hold for 4 counts
Relax your body, exhale your breath, and take a quick breathe without getting tense. Keep the throat open and expand from the diaphragm.
Take a deep breath and play a mid-range note for as many seconds as you can
Play a three note pattern ascending and descending all in one breath without articulating. Try repeating the pattern several times. Pick new notes at different pitch levels each day.

The placement and pressure of the lips on the beak of the recorder is also paramount to creating good tone. The lips should be relaxed and loose, but not so loose that air is leaked out of the sides. It is important not to grip the instrument with the lips, but simply place the lips around the beak in a forward, "O" shape. The teeth should not touch the recorder at all.

To ensure continuous progression of tone quality, the best exercises to play when you begin practicing are long tones. **Long tones** are notes played at longer durations, such as whole notes (4 counts), or longer. This allows us to focus on breath and **embouchure** in order to produce long, beautiful tones. Here are a few examples of long tone exercises for recorders in "C" and for recorders in "F".

Long Tones for Recorder in "C"

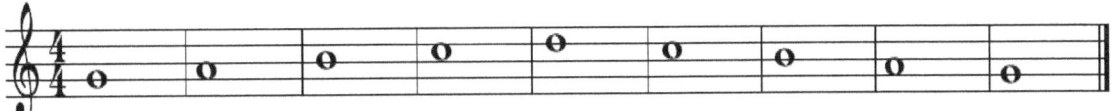

Long Tones for Recorder in "F"

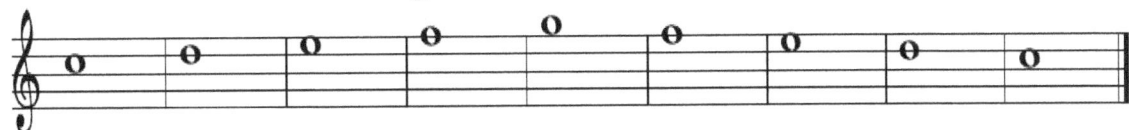

Initially, when practicing tone on the recorder, it is best to focus on notes that are not in the extreme ranges. Starting with notes that are easier to play will allow you to focus on the embouchure (formation of lips), air speed, and air direction. For recorders in "C", the range of "G-D" is a great mid-range to begin with, and for recorders in "F", the range "C-G" is best, which uses the same fingers. How high or low the note is will influence the speed of the air being used. The mid-range notes will require a steady, medium paced air stream.

To assess if the tone you are producing is of good quality, listen to the resonance and steadiness of the note. Resonance describes how full, deep, and reverberating the sound is. One may describe resonance as how the sound "rings" pleasantly in the ear. The steadiness of the note is measured by how it maintains a constant, unwavering tone. Focus on the resonance and steadiness of the sound when playing long tones. If the sound is unsteady, adjust the speed of the air you are using and ensure the air is flowing consistently. To improve resonance, maintain a loose embouchure and keep the face and body relaxed.

Low vs. High Notes

As previously mentioned, low notes and high notes require different air speeds to create the ideal tones. For low notes, the air stream needs to be slow and gentle.

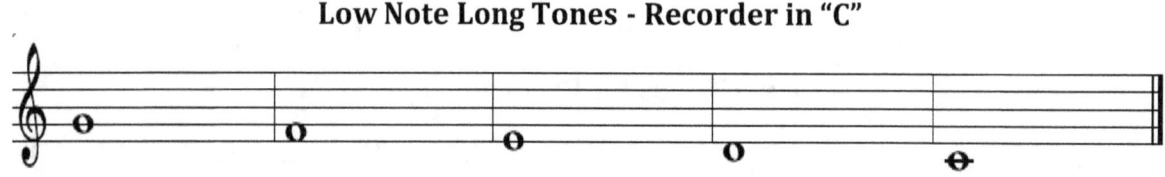

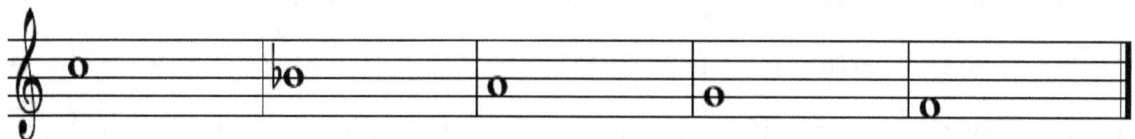

High notes require a faster air stream. The tongue can also assist with achieving the right air pressure for high notes. A decisive articulation will assist the air in moving quickly into the recorder so that the high note speaks, or responds, immediately.

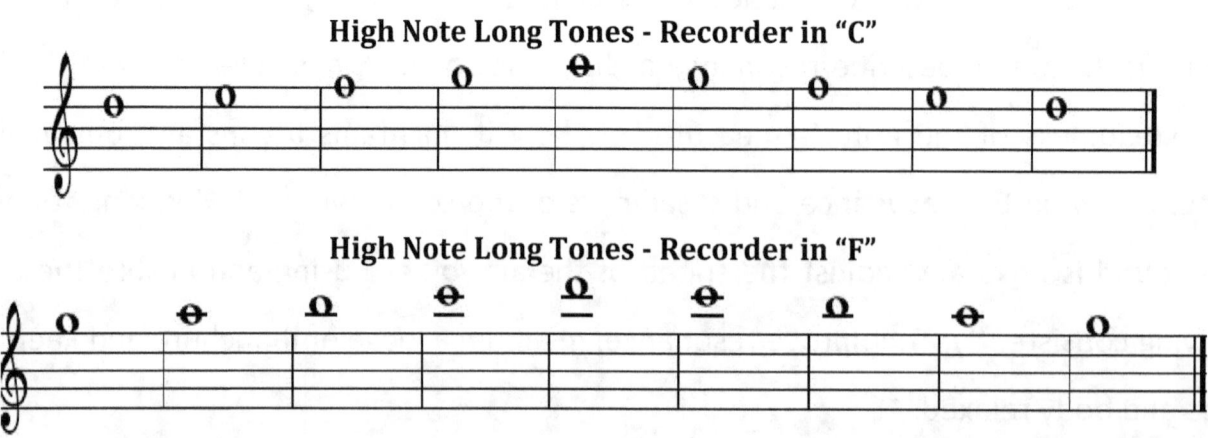

Intonation

In music, **intonation** is the accuracy of the note or pitch in regards to it being at the correct frequency. This means that the note is sounding in a way that is not too high or low for the sound the note is supposed to produce. When playing an instrument like the recorder, it is possible to play the note too high or low without actually changing notes. For example, when playing the note "B" on recorders in "C", or "E" on recorders in "F", it is possible to push this note higher or lower without moving the fingers to a different position. This is done by either blowing too hard or not blowing hard enough.

When a note is too high, it is said that the note is "too sharp". This is not the same as sharp signs and semitones. A note that is sharp in relation to tuning is out of tune because it is higher than the note should be. When a note is too low, it is said that the note is "too flat." This is not the same as a flat sign or semitone. When determining intonation, a note being too flat just means it is lower than the note is intended to be, and is sounding at a lower frequency.

It can take months to years of ear training to be able distinguish intonation on your instrument. Luckily, there is a tool that musicians use that can measure whether you are playing a note at the correct frequency. This tool is called a **tuner**, and it can be found as an electronic device, or as an application for smartphones. A tuner will pick up the note you are playing and measure its frequency. The display will indicate if the note is too low (flat) or too high (sharp), typically using a digital needle along with corresponding lights. The goal is to get the indicator to be in the center.

If you are producing a lovely, steady, resonant sound on a mid-range note of your recorder and it is out of tune, there is a way to adjust the recorder itself. First, the temperature of the instrument influences intonation. If the instrument has not been played before tuning, it may be a little cold, which causes flatness. Warm-up the recorder by either playing a few long tones and scales, or warm it with your hands by wrapping them around the recorder. Some players also put the recorder under their arm and hold it against their body to increase the temperature.

If your recorder is warmed and reading sharp, we may need to adjust the instrument. To adjust for sharpness, pull the head joint of your recorder out slightly from the body without removing it. By lengthening the recorder, we've adjusted it to sound slightly lower. To adjust for flatness, be sure that the head joint is pushed in all the way, meeting the body without any space in the joint. This shortens the recorder to adjust the sound higher. If you play a mid-range note after adjusting the head joint accordingly, and you've regulated the temperature, but the recorder is still out of tune, your recorder may need structural adjustments and needs to be evaluated by a professional.

A tuner allows you to visually see how close the pitch is to the exact frequency predetermined by a system called equal temperament. Equal temperament is the dividing of the frequency of all semitones within an octave, equally. This is how instruments like the piano and harp are tuned since their notes are set to a fixed frequency that cannot be changed while playing. The recorder, by contrast, is flexible with tuning each note. Like the human voice, the frequency of a note can be changed in the midst of playing. This means that it is essential to train the ears to hear when things are in tune or out of tune.

In order to learn to tune by ear, you will need an additional, external note being sounded with which to tune. This could be an additional instrument, or there are recordings of notes on YouTube and some tuning devices. To start, play the same note along with the external sound. When two notes are sounded simultaneously, the frequencies of the sounds interact and will sound like one, smooth sound if in tune. There will be beats or waves in the sound if they are not in tune with each other. The goal is to adjust the frequency of your pitch to match the other sound. This is done by adjusting the air pressure to bring the note up or down to the frequency of the other pitch.

Pitches of differing frequencies can be tuned as well. This takes extensive ear training to listen and hear if two differing notes are locking in to the correct frequencies. Learning to adjust intonation to any interval or chord is essential when playing in a recorder **ensemble** or **consort**. It is also important to solo playing since most solo recorder music is accompanied by an additional instrument such as the piano or harpsichord.

Scales and Key Signatures

While long tones develop the beauty in the sound you are creating, there are also exercises to practice that develop your finger speed and accuracy. The most universally used of these patterns are scales. A scale, in music, is defined as any graduated sequence of notes, tones, or intervals, typically dividing an octave. For beginners, it is best to begin exploration and practice of scales with the **major** and **minor scales** for their instrument.

Major scales are a pleasant, happy sounding sequence in a stepwise ascending and descending pattern. There is a major scale for every pitch class (the musical alphabet plus the sharp/flat notes), so twelve in total.

$$A, A\#/B\flat, B, C, C\#/D\flat, D, D\#/E\flat, E, F, F\#/G\flat, G, G\#/A\flat$$

At first, you should practice each of these scales starting in the first octave (lower note) of that pitch class, and later expand into the higher octaves and multi-octave scales. The suggested order to approach practicing scales is starting with the least amount of flats and sharps required to play the scale. All major scales are included at the end of this guide in the suggested order for practice.

Minor scales are often described as sounding sad or spooky. Like major scales, they are also a stepwise ascending and descending pattern of eight notes, and there is a minor scale for every pitch class. The difference is in the sequence of notes for each pitch class. While C Major has no flats or sharps in the scale, C minor has three flats. This means that C minor and E♭ Major share the flatted notes, but they are not the same scale because the order of the letters is not the same. Major and minor scales that share the same accidentals are called relative scales. There is a relative minor for every major scale. Minor scales for both recorder in "C" and recorder in "F" are found along with their relative major scales in the final section of this guide.

When music is written, it typically follows a structure that is built based upon a scale. Whatever scale this is, the first note is like the home note of the scale, and the piece or section of music will be at least mostly based on this scale. The technical term for this home note of the scale is the **tonic**. The tonic determines the **key** of the musical selection. This means that a piece of music could be in one of twelve major keys or one of twelve minor keys. Many works from the Classical and Baroque Era of music reference the key of the music in the title. For example, there is the "Sonata in F Major" by J.S. Bach.

Rather than have the flats and sharps written on every note needed to fit a specific scale, the flats and sharps are gathered at the beginning of every line of music in a notation called the **key signature**. The key signature is found right after the treble clef at the beginning of any piece of recorder music. If there are not any flats or sharps grouped here, then the key signature is the key of C Major or A minor because these scales require no flats or sharps.

The flats or sharps in a key signature will be written on the line or space of the note to be altered and apply to all notes of the indicated pitch class. For example, in the key of F

Major or D minor, there is one flat in the key signature. This flat is on the third line of the staff, which is where the note "B" is notated in treble clef. This key signature indicates that all "B's" are to be played as "B♭" in the subsequent music following the key signature. While there is a key signature found at the beginning of a piece of music, the key can be changed within the music. When this occurs, the new set of flats or sharps will be indicated at that point of the key change, and the new key takes effect for the music following that point.

Natural signs are used on occasion to cancel a sharp or flat from the key signature. Sharp and flat signs that are not in the key signature can also be added to notes. When this occurs, any sharp, flat, or natural sign that is not in the key signature is considered an **accidental**.

This **Circle of Fifths** displays all major and minor key signatures in ascending order of number of sharps on the right side, and in ascending order of number of flats on the left side. Notice that for both sharps and flats, there is an order or sequence in which they are listed. The key signatures with multiple flats or sharps are more challenging to play for most players. For beginners, it is best to begin learning music in the keys of C Major/A Minor, G Major/E Minor, and F Major/D Minor. To prepare for these pieces, practice scales in those keys.

You may wonder how to determine if the key is in major or minor, since relative major and minor scales share the same accidentals. This ultimately depends on how the notes of the music are arranged and sequenced. Sometimes the title of the music will include the key (i.e. "Sonata in E Minor"), but if not, a little analyzing may reveal the answer. If the note patterns seem to center around, lead to, or settle onto a particular note, it is likely that note is the key center. Also, our ears can hear if a piece of music is major or minor once we've grown accustomed to those sounds. Listen to music in various major and minor keys, and practice both types of scales to build the skills to distinguish the two.

To expand even further upon the practice of scales, there are three possible forms of the minor scale. The key signature will not be affected when altering notes to create these minor scales. Rather than the key signature being affected, particular notes of the scale could have an accidental not found in the key signature. The three forms of minor are **natural minor, harmonic minor**, and **melodic minor**.

The natural minor scale is played without any alterations or accidentals that are not found in the key signature. Music in natural minor will not have many accidentals and will abide mostly by the key signature.

The harmonic scale raises the seventh note of the scale by a half step, creating an altered pattern and sound. The raising of this pitch will be done with an accidental on the note. It will usually be a sharp of a natural sign on the seventh note of the scale. The harmonic minor scale is the most commonly used form of minor.

The melodic minor scale is unique. A few of the notes in the ascending scale differ from the descending scale. In melodic minor, the sixth and seventh pitches are raised by a half step when the scale is descending. So, it is a natural minor scale going up, but altered going down.

Familiarity with scales and key signatures will develop fluidity with note patterns that will be seen in music. Initially, practice scales slowly until you can play them smoothly and steadily. Incrementally increase the speed, and eventually vary the articulations. Articulation is the way we use our tongue to start notes and will be discussed in the next portion of this guide.

Expression

Once the technicalities have been established, the player should explore adding **expression** to their playing. Playing with expression encompasses adding volume, articulation varieties, and interpretation to your playing that will create interest, style, and emotion in the music. Expressive techniques and elements are used to shape the musical line and bring the music to life.

Dynamics

Dynamics are the louds and softs of music, or to put it simply, the volume. These markings are found in music to give guidance to how loud or soft a musical passage should be played. Let's begin with the core dynamic markings.

pp	pianissimo	very soft
p	piano	soft
mp	mezzo piano	moderately soft
mf	mezzo forte	moderately loud
f	forte	loud
ff	fortissimo	very loud

There are two approaches to create soft sounds on the recorder. One way is with alternate fingerings for notes. These alternate fingerings will change the fingerings you use to play the soft notes in music. This method is only really practical when being used for a longer soft passage. The alternate fingerings do slightly change the tone color of the sound and the intonation, and will need to be compensated for with air pressure accordingly.

The second method that can be used to play softly on the recorder is "**leaking**" air from one of the covered tone holes of a note. To leak a tone hole, the finger will open the hole a very minimal amount to allow a tiny amount of air to leak. Only one finger needs to leak to play softly. Some players prefer to leak the lowest finger of a note, meaning the finger furthest toward the bottom of the recorder. Any finger can be leaked to achieve the softening effect. Most find that the most practical approach is to leak the first finger on tone hole 1. Training this finger will apply to a majority of notes, since most notes involve covering tone hole 1. When the hole is leaked, the pitch will raise and go sharp. The player must pull back the air pressure to compensate for this sharpness. Once the leaking and air pressure are evened out, a soft, in tune sound can be produced.

To leak the tone hole with the finger properly, the finger must press into the recorder in order to roll a small amount downward. Let's practice the leaking technique with a "G" on recorders in "C" or a "C" on recorders in "F". These notes involve covering tone holes 0, 1, 2, 3 on either recorder. We are going to leak the first finger in this exercise. Make certain you have a good hand position and press the first finger into the recorder. Then, slightly roll it downward in order to create a tiny opening at the top of tone hole 1. As you open the tone hole, you will need to adjust the breath pressure. If you continue blowing with the same pressure, the note will pop up into a high note rather than soften. Try this technique on several notes to achieve soft playing on multiple notes.

The thumb hole can also be leaked to different degrees to aid soft playing. When the leaked opening is smaller, the sound will be stronger. To engage soft playing, allow the thumb to open the hole further and decrease the air pressure.

Basically, to play softly involves using less air pressure and adjusting the pitch through either alternate fingerings or leaking. To play louder, the opposite will be true. We need to use more or faster air pressure, which without adjustment, will cause the sound to go sharp. To compensate for this, there are two general techniques to lower the pitch when blowing harder to achieve louder sound.

First, adding space inside the mouth will lower the pitch and allow you to blow faster air. Players describe this sensation as "widening" the inside of the mouth to create more space inside the oral cavity. This gives the recorder a robust, brassier tone that is perceived as louder.

The second technique is called "**shading**". Shading is like the reverse of leaking. Rather than opening an already covered tone hole like we do to leak, we can begin to cover an already open tone hole to shade. If the tone hole is further away from the desired fingering, it can even be completely covered if going for a straightforward loud note. For example, if playing the note "B" on recorders in "C" ("E" on recorders in "F"), we can play louder by blowing harder and keep it in tune by closing tone hole 4. We can also use the shading technique by approaching any tone hole that is uncovered without actually closing it. To shade the note, the finger will hover above the tone hole as if approaching to close it, but never sealing the hole. The closer to the top of the recorder the shaded tone hole is, the more effect it will have on the pitch.

For notes that already cover most or all of the tone holes, we can shade the end of the recorder to lower the pitch. This is done by bringing the end of the recorder toward the knee without completely closing the hole.

In music, dynamics are all relative to each other. For notes to be perceived as soft, the preceding notes should be played more loudly in contrast, and vice versa. There are also dynamic markings that indicate gradual changes in dynamics. The most widely used of these markings are the **crescendo** and **decrescendo**.

cresc. _ _ _ _ _   *dim.* _ _ _ _ _ _ _

A crescendo indicates to gradually get louder by increasing the volume. On recorder, this can be done by increasing air pressure along with the shading technique. As the finger gets closer to the hole to be shaded, the player can increase their breath pressure to get louder. The shading is used to keep the sound in tune. As the breath pressure increases, the finger should get closer to the tone hole it is shading.

A decrescendo (also commonly called a **diminuendo**) indicates to gradually get softer by decreasing the volume. On recorder, this is achieved by decreasing the air pressure along with the leaking technique. As the finger opens the tone hole to leak, the player can decrease their breath pressure to get a softer sound and stay in tune. As the breath pressure decreases, the finger can roll to open or leak the tone hole.

Gaining control and consistency over dynamic changes will take practice and experimentation. When attempting dynamic changes, always listen for the differences in tone and pitch as adjustments are made. The goal is to maintain a resonant, steady, in tune sound at any dynamic level.

Vibrato

The term **vibrato** is derived from the Italian word "vibrare", which means to vibrate. Vibrato is a musical effect that involves the intentional pulsing the pitch. To create vibrato, the pitch is pushed up and down at a regular, equal rate. This causes the sound to waver in pitch up and down, creating vibrato. Vibrato is a useful tool in adding expression to your playing. Vibrato can fluctuate at different speeds for various effects. For example, a fast, narrow vibrato is perceived differently than a slow, wide vibrato.

Before discovering your vibrato, a straight tone must be established. Straight tone refers to the smooth, steady sound without any fluctuation. This straight, full tone will be used as the basis. Let's visualize this as a straight line.

———————————————

Vibrato is the fluctuation of this straight tone without totally leaving it. The curved line below visualizes how the fluctuation will rise above and fall below the straight line at equal distances and a steady rate.

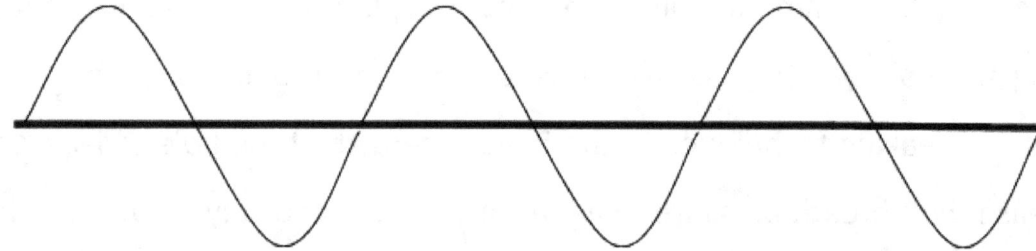

Vibrato can be created using our air or our fingers. We will focus on air/ breath vibrato first. To start applying breath or air vibrato to the recorder, there are two useful techniques. One begins by holding a straight tone and then letting it fall by decreasing your air using a mid-range note. Then do the opposite. Start with little air and increase the air, going upward into a straight tone. Then connect the two slowly to create waves in the sound. It should sound almost like a siren going up and down. Continuously increase the speed of this fluctuation, and you will have a resemblance of vibrato.

The second technique uses laughing to emulate the feeling of fluctuating the air. Say "ha, ha, ha" as if you are laughing. Now do the same, without vocalizing. You should feel the air fluctuate as you pretend to laugh. Now, begin with a straight tone on a mid-range note, and then use the fake laughing sensation to fluctuate the pitch. Be sure that your embouchure and body remain relaxed. Experiment with different speeds to vary your vibrato, and continue to experiment and practice on multiple notes.

Once you've found your vibrato, you can begin honing it to gain control over the rate and depth. Vibrato has two components, the rate, or speed, and the depth, or amplitude. Understanding how to control both will allow the ultimate flexibility in expressive use of your vibrato. Start by counting out a slow, steady four count beat. Then, add vibrato to beats two and four. To begin with, add two fluctuations or waves to the sound between the straight tones in between. Increase the waves or fluctuations little by little to continue developing faster vibrato. The table below lays out a vibrato exercise over four counts. The columns indicate the count to play straight versus adding vibrato, and the rows indicate how many waves or fluctuations of vibrato are being added on beats two and four.

–	Straight	*Vibrato*	Straight	*Vibrato*
2 waves	1 - &	2 - &	3 - &	4 - &
3 waves	1 - *la* - *lee*	2 - *la* - *lee*	3 - *la* - *lee*	4 - *la* - *lee*
4 waves	1 - e - & - *a*	2 - e - & - *a*	3 - e - & - *a*	4 - e - & - *a*

To practice changing how wide, or the amplitude of the vibrato, play a four count tone. Start with a narrow vibrato and increasingly widen it for two counts, and then come back to narrow for two counts.

All of the aforementioned vibrato techniques are focused on developing the air vibrato, which will be your primary choice of vibrato. A secondary type of vibrato uses your fingers to fluctuate the sound and is often referred to as finger vibrato. The technical term is flattement, which is a French technique of using specific trill fingerings to create vibrato. This is considered an extended technique for recorder and will be discussed later in this guide.

Once you've experimented with these techniques and activated air and vibrato, the best way to continue honing your skills is to play a slow, beautiful song. Expressive elements of playing such as vibrato also involve our own physical and musical intuition. Really listen to your playing and the music and add vibrato where you find to be most appealing.

Articulation

The term articulation encompasses all of the markings and techniques that can be used to vary how the start of each note is approached. When we articulate a note, we are using our tongue to begin the note. When you first started playing, this guide instructed you to use a "du" tongue to begin each sound. This is a generic, undefined articulation to get the player started. There are various techniques to articulate notes. The way the tongue approaches each note can contribute to the expression in our playing.

The tongue can be used to control the length of a note, without changing the rhythm. For example, quarter notes can be played with a shorter articulation that creates separation between the notes, or they can be played more fully with little separation. The shortest articulation markings in music are **staccato** and **staccatissimo**.

Staccato   Staccatissimo

The syllables the tongue will emulate to create staccato and staccatissimo are "dot" and "dit." When you say the words "dot" or "dit", the tongue starts and stops the word. When using a "dot" or "dit" tongue, the start of each note is the same as our original "du" tongue. This time, however, there is a stop to the end of the note. Staccatissimo is the shortest, most detached articulation and uses a "dit" tongue. Staccato is slightly longer and uses "dot".

On the opposite of the spectrum from staccato is legato tonguing. Legato style indicates smooth and connected, without any separation between the notes. Legato is the absence of articulation, as the air continuously flows as the fingers change notes with no interference from the tongue. The marking that represents **legato** playing is called a **slur**. In a group of notes or passages with slurs, the first note at the beginning of the slur is tongued using a "du" tongue. Any notes under the slur will not be tongued, and the air must continuously flow as the fingers manipulate the notes in the group or passage.

Legato

While legato is the extremity of long articulation, there are markings that indicate sustaining the note to its full rhythmic value with minimal, gentle separation between the notes. In a large amount of recorder repertoire, this is called **portato**. Portato is also called articulated legato. The notes are still to be played smooth and connected, but with the tongue entering just long enough to begin each note. The marking that indicates portato is the slur and staccato dots combined.

Portato

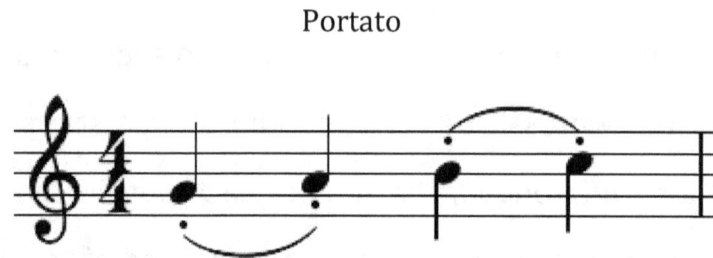

In some instances, the **tenuto** marking is used to indicate a similar articulation style to portato. This horizontal line is most often interpreted to indicate that the note be played full length with slight separation between the notes, like portato. Some composers and musicians, however, have used this marking to also indicate slight dynamic emphasis as well. How the musical line lends itself to shaping and the player's personal preferences and interpretation of the music influence to what extent markings are to be expressed.

Tenuto

So far, the articulations we've analyzed have had influence on the length of the note. Articulation can also vary in strength based on the consonant with which the player approaches the note. In recorder, "T", "D", "R", and "L" are used to vary the strength the tongue uses to start a note. They are listed in order from strongest to weakest, "T", "D", "R", and "L". When varying the intensity with which you articulate, the air stream should remain consistent. The strength comes from the tongue using these consonants to offer different degrees of intensity to the start of a note. Experiment with starting notes using each of these consonants and listen for how they influence the start of each note. Remember, the tongue should be hitting right where the roof of your mouth meets the back of the top row of teeth.

In music, there are articulation markings that guide the player in both the strength and length intended for a note or group of notes. **Accent** and **marcato** marking both indicate to play with a more explosive articulation, which on the recorder would use the consonant "T". Accents indicate longer sustain and are often described as 75% of the note's total rhythmic value, using a "Tah" tonguing syllable. Marcato markings indicate a shorter note with a stop, like staccato, but with a more aggressive start to the note. While staccato uses a "dit" tongue, marcato uses "tit."

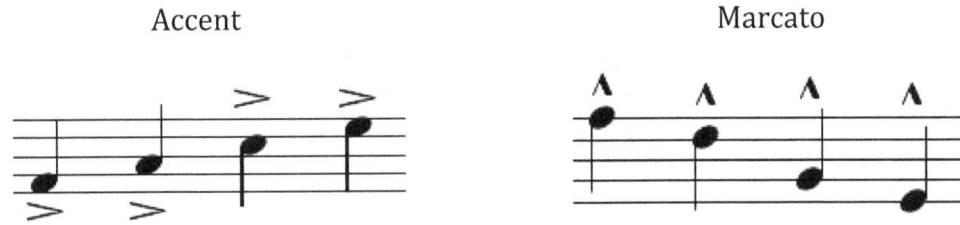

Markings aside, using the tongue to add expression to your playing also involves the player's musical interpretation, taking into account the style and time period of the music being played. For example if there was a piece of music without any articulation markings. This wouldn't indicate to leave out any articulation styles. The articulation should still be varied in order to shape and express the musical line.

Interpretation

Now that you've built the knowledge and skills required to begin adding expression to your playing, let's discuss elements that guide our expressive decisions. We've mentioned on a few occasions in this position of the guide that the individual's interpretation and preferences play a part in playing expressively. If you were to listen to the exact same piece of music performed by different people, they would not sound exactly the same. This is because music is free and organic in the way, allowing us to put our own interpretations into what we are playing. There are a few things to consider, however, when applying expressive elements to a musical composition.

In common performance practice, the composer and time period in which a piece of music was written guides the expression of experienced players. When playing a musical composition, the composer's original intent should be taken into account in interpreting the music. For example, a staccato marking in music from the Classical Era would imply a short, light, fluffy detachment, while a staccato in modern, contemporary music might be more pointed and clipped. In addition to the historical context, how the musical line is written can guide the player in shaping the line appropriately. Listening to professional performers and reading about music history in relation to the time periods of music will help guide your interpretation and expression.

Ornaments

Ornaments are like musical decorations. Notes that are not essential to the melody or harmony can be added to a musical line to add interest and variety to the music. Think of musical ornaments as embellishments - the line can be carried out without them, but the use of them may decorate and enhance the music.

The type of ornament and how it is performed varies by style and time period of music. In the Baroque Era of music, performers commonly improvised their own embellishments over a melodic line to add variety, interest, and to show off virtuosic playing. Many composers also notated ornaments in the music, but the approach to these notations has varied over time. For the purposes of this guide, we will focus on the most widely applicable definitions and descriptions of some of the most commonly seen ornamentations found in recorder music. To further understand how to add and interpret ornamentation of a certain time period, listen to recorder music in the style of music you are working on or wish to learn. Listening suggestions will also be included along the way.

Trills

A **trill** is a rapid alteration of an indicated note and the note directly above that note. It is a common ornament used in music for woodwind instruments. If you were to close tone holes 0, 1, 2 on your recorder and then rapidly open and close tone hole 2 while blowing, you would create a trill between "A" and "B" on recorders in "C", or "D" and "E" on recorders in "F".

There are several symbols used to notate trills found in music. In music from the Baroque Era, a plus sign above the note to be trilled is most common. In modern music, the abbreviation "tr" sometimes followed by a squiggly line is used.

As previously stated, trills alternate between the note indicated and the note above the indicated note. Whether the note above is natural or altered by a sharp or flat differs. For example, a trill marked on the note "G" could indicate to trill up to "A" or "A♭". Or a trill marked on the note "E" could indicate to trill up to "F" or "F♯". This is usually determined by the key signature. If there were an "A♭" in the key signature, then the "G" would alternate up to "A♭". If there were an "F♯" in the key signature, then the "E" would alternate up to "F♯". Always check the key signature when determining how to play a trill.

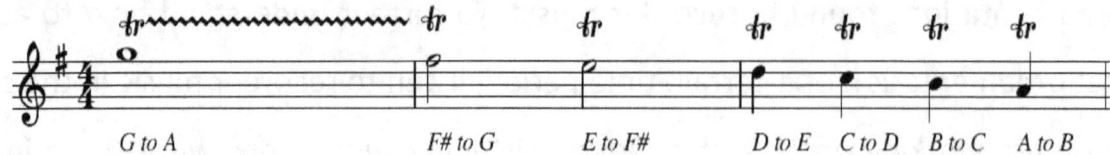

G to A   F# to G   E to F#   D to E   C to D   B to C   A to B

There are occurrences of trills in which the intended upper note may note adhere to the key signature. In these cases, a flat or sharp sign will be printed along with the trill indication, typically above the staff.

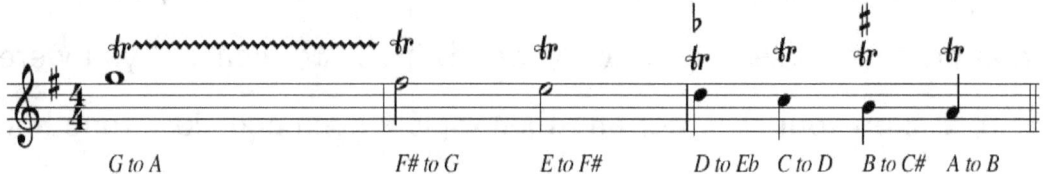

G to A   F# to G   E to F#   D to Eb   C to D   B to C#   A to B

During the Baroque Era, a trill was approached in a specific way, that since has become common practice. When playing music from the Baroque Era or in the Baroque style, it is assumed to begin the trill on the upper note. This means that you would play the alteration of the indicated note before the printed note, and then continuing to alternate rapidly between the two notes. So, if there were a trill indicated on a "C", you would first play "D" (or "D♭" if the key signature were to contain it) and then begin alternating between "C" and "D" for the duration of the note.

Mordents

A similar marking to a trill, a **mordent** is also a rapid alternation between two pitches. In its original intent, a mordent is one quick fluctuation between the note on which it is indicated and the note below that note. The marking for this type of mordent is a short squiggly line with a vertical line through the middle.

This can be inverted to go the other way around, meaning that the indicated note is quickly alternated with the note above it. This is technically an inverted mordent. The marking for an inverted mordent is the short squiggly line without the vertical line.

These markings are often referred to as lower mordent and upper mordent to more clearly distinguish the direction of the alteration. Mordents also adhere to the key signature to determine what note to alternate the indicated note. With either upper or lower mordents, the indicated note is played first, then quickly altered up or down depending if it's an upper or lower mordent, and finally returns to the original printed note.

Glissando/Portamento

Often called a slide or bend, a **glissando** and/or **portamento** are a unique musical effect created by ascending or descending between two specified notes in a special manner. In most music, a glissando indicates to play every note possible between the two pitches in rapid succession. This would include all of the half steps, or sharps and flats, along the way. It is often notated as a straight line, a squiggly line, the abbreviation gliss., or a both the line and text.

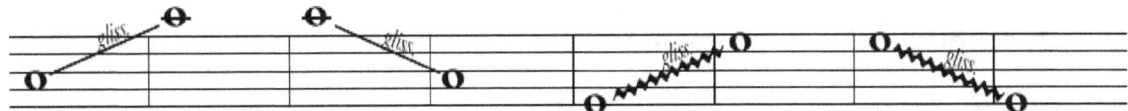

A portamento creates a similarly musical effect, but at the smoothest degree. A portamento is an ascending or descending slide between two indicated pitches. While a glissando includes every half step between two pitches, a portamento technically encompasses every pitch frequency level between two pitches. Basically, this means that every pitch level possible will be created in one fluid duration between notes.

While there is a distinct difference in most definitions of glissando and portamento, there are of course contradictions as well. These terms are used interchangeably in recorder music, and also called slides or bends. A glissando in recorder music will be played as a portamento. It will be notated similarly to the glissando markings, but with perhaps the word portamento or the abbreviation "port." This is partially because the recorder is one of few instruments capable of producing a true portamento slide. In this guide, we will discuss how to play a recorder glissando/portamento in its most widely accepted form, a slide.

It is best to begin practicing with an ascending glissando/portamento. To achieve the effect of bending the pitch upward, each finger will be either pulling or rolling slowly away or off of its tone hole. This will occur in a particular order that is dependent upon which two pitches the glissando/portamento is between. The first note indicated in the glissando/portamento will be where your fingers begin. Fingers will be removed from the recorder from highest to lowest, or top to bottom, until the next indicated note is reached.

Let's attempt a glissando/portamento between the first octave "G" to "A" on recorder in "C", and "C" to "D" on recorder in "F". You will start with your fingers covering tone holes 0, 1, 2, 3. This glissando/portamento will require removing finger 3 from tone hole 3. The glissando/portamento can be performed using a couple of different techniques. One option is to slowly pull the finger away and off of the tone hole. A second option is to roll; your finger above or below the tone hole, and you can even roll toward the opposite side of your hand. The direction in which you pull or roll your finger slightly influences how the glissando/portamento is produced. You may wish to experiment to find the method and sound you prefer. Many players find that pulling the finger away from the hole to be the easiest way to get a smooth glide between notes. The objective is to create a slide between the two pitches without arriving or departing too abruptly.

A descending glissando or portamento requires the player to slowly and gradually add fingers to cover tone holes. Many find this more challenging than removing fingers. Take the same two notes from the preceding paragraph. For recorders in "C", we are going to glissando/portamento from the second octave "A" to "G", which is "D" to "C" on recorders in "F". This time, the finger will need to slowly approach and cover the hole little by little. We do not want the pitch to change abruptly. The objective is to again get the smooth, gliding sound between the notes.

A glissando/portamento can be found in music between notes of small to larger distances apart on the staff. The further apart they are, the more challenges they may pose to achieve smoothly. When multiple fingers are involved, they must depart or arrive on the tone holes in a particular order. Which fingers ultimately depends on the two notes indicated in the glissando/portamento. When deciphering a glissando/portamento, determine the sequence of fingers by stepping the fingers up or down the recorder like a scale, starting with the first indicated note and ending with the second indicated note.

Notes that are in separate octaves, such as a first octave note to a second octave note, require extremely advanced technique to achieve. To further study and practice the most advanced recorder techniques and ornaments, such as glissandi spanning over octaves, an advanced teacher may recommend specialized method books for you at that point in your playing.

Additional Information

Troubleshooting

It is inevitable that while you are learning how to play the recorder, you will experience issues in your playing. Some of these issues you may be able to solve easily, such as blowing too hard or too lightly, using improper hand position, or playing incorrect notes. You will likely also encounter issues that you can't identify what is going wrong. In these instances, you will have to do some troubleshooting to rule out what is or is not the cause of the issue.

Leaky Fingers

First, a common beginner mistake is leaky fingers. This is done unintentionally and may cause squeaks or incorrect pitches. It is important that your fingers seal all of the tone holes required for the note you are playing. The more fingers a note requires, the more room for error. For example, if you are working on playing a low note and feel you have the proper breath pressure and speed, but the note is still note right, check that all of the required fingers are truly sealing the entirety of their assigned tone hole. This may solve the issue easily and is commonly the culprit.

Poor Posture

Because playing an instrument requires abundant multi-talking (breathing, air pressure, reading music, tonguing, hand position, sealing tone holes, listening, etc.), it is essential that you continue to review the basics at the beginning of every practice session. The one thing that tends to be neglected the most is posture. If you notice that your back, wrists, or hands are experiencing pain or stiffness during or after playing, this may be because of poor posture or hand position. Also, if you feel that you don't have enough breath to play through multiple counts of notes, you may be playing with poor posture. Unless you practice regularly in the mirror, you may not notice that you are slouching when you are concentrating on the various other concepts you practice. Ideally, check your posture regularly when preparing to play and in the midst of your practice sessions. Breaks between songs or exercises are also great opportunities to check in on your posture.

Over Breathing

If you feel that when you play, your sound is choppy or unconnected, pay attention to your air and how it flows into the recorder. Many beginners will subconsciously breathe between every note, causing a huffy, disjunct sound to the music. When playing, remember to keep a steady air stream. The tongue is used to begin notes, unless slurs are marked, and should simply interrupt the air stream, and not stop it. The air stream should continue to flow steadily until the player takes a new breath. To practice this without the recorder, say "du-du-du-du-du" all on one breath. Avoid taking a new breath until finished. Now try the same on a singular note on the recorder. Keep this technique in mind whenever playing music to avoid breathing before every note.

Depending on what size your recorder is, you may find that you have too much air while you're playing. This may become evident if you have to exhale between notes or are exhaling through your nose while playing. The smaller the instrument, the less air required to play. Adjust the volume of your inhalation to the instrument you are playing to use your air efficiently and avoid excess tension in your body.

Dropped Notes

If you are playing music on your recorder and you notice that the ends of notes are bending in pitch, or going flat, there is an easy adjustment to be made. The dropping at the end of notes is due to the air stream not remaining constant. The air needs to stay steady right up to the end of the note, and not sooner. This will clean up your playing immensely and keep your notes in tune.

Throat Articulation

Many beginners struggle with learning to use their tongue to properly begin notes. One of the most common tonguing mistakes is not tonguing at all. It is possible to start a note by simply blowing without any "du" tongue. This will create a sloppier beginning to the note that is unclear and often out of tune. Alternatively, some players will start the note using their throat. This is extremely unhealthy for your voice box and mustn't be used. If you find that you are articulating with your throat, break that habit immediately by practicing "du" tonguing on simple patterns and repeated notes. A final tonguing mistake to avoid is using or moving the whole tongue to articulate. Only the tip of the tongue should be used to begin a note.

Biting

Finally, if you are experiencing tension in your jaw, cheeks, or mouth, you might be biting your recorder. The teeth should never touch the recorder for a few reasons. First, it will damage the mouthpiece over time. If you've been biting, you may notice teeth marks appear on the top of your instrument. Second, biting leads to tension in the mouth and jaw, which is also bad for you. Players that have poor posture and/or hand position will tend to bite in order to feel like they have control and balance of the instrument. The solution to holding the recorder is never biting. Proper posture and hand position will balance the recorder properly so that biting is not necessary.

Tips and Tricks

The following is a list of hacks that may be useful as you continue building upon your recorder knowledge.

1. Cleaning hack: When choosing a cloth with which to clean out the moisture inside your instrument, it is recommended to use a smooth, cotton cloth. Instrument retailers sell these fluffy, stick cleaning apparatuses that oftentimes shed inside the instrument and fall apart. Many professional recorder players use a cut-up cotton t-shirt, handkerchief, or even a sock laced through a cleaning rod to swab out the inside of the instrument after playing to rid of excess moisture.

2. Practice hack: Regular practice is essential to your success on the recorder. However, if you live with or in close proximity to other people, you may need a way to practice more quietly on occasion. This can be done very easily using a small, folded up strip of paper. The window and labium of the recorder is where the sound is created, and by gently and carefully inserting a small piece of paper, you can create a practice mute for your instrument. You can still "play" the recorder, and practice blowing, fingerings, and articulations, but there won't be much sound. This should not be used regularly, but it can be useful when you need to practice quietly.

3. Thumb placement: Beginners and young students often have trouble placing the right thumb on the back of the recorder. As mentioned early in the guide when we discussed hand placement, the right thumb should be placed behind tone hole 5. The player may initially place it accurately, but as you play it may migrate up or down the recorder and lead to poor hand position habits. To avoid this, a small sticker or round piece of felt can be fastened to the correct place to give the thumb a surface to anchor upon.

4. Thumb rest: When playing a larger recorder such as the tenor recorder, or any recorder for long durations, the weight of the instrument can cause strain on your hands. Thumb rests are great for alleviating some of this stress and ensuring proper balance when holding and playing the instrument. People with smaller hands may find thumb rests necessary to not strain their hands and wrists. Thumb rests are purchasable as an attachment to the recorder. Some larger recorders have a thumb rest built in, and can also be installed by a professional recorder crafter. Whether you install a permanent thumb rest or attach a removable thumb rest, it is important that it is placed correctly.

5. Slings and Harnesses: For very large recorders such as the bass recorder, a sling around the neck can be hooked on the back of the recorder to carry the weight of the instrument. If you have shoulder or neck problems, a body harness can be used the same way. Make sure to purchase adjustable slings and harnesses so you can achieve proper hand placement.

6. Thread Hack: Recorders without cork on the joints can also be sealed using thread. Thread can be wound around the joint to create thickness so that the joints are not loose and seal properly. The best technique for threading is to do so in a criss-cross-manner. This will require less thread and optimize the seal of the joints.

Solo Recorder vs. Duets, Trios, and Recorder Consorts

For centuries, music has been written for both solo instruments and voices as well as ensembles. Music for a solo instrument is written for a single person to play or sing, oftentimes with a second instrument serving as accompaniment. For example, a recorder solo may include piano accompaniment. Common instruments used for accompaniment in recorder music are piano and harpsichord. Although an additional instrument part may be featured as an accompaniment, the music is considered a recorder solo because the recorder is the melody, or main part of the piece. Music written without accompaniment is specified as unaccompanied.

Most solo music for recorder is written for the soprano and alto recorders. Solos for any instrument can be found in many forms. There are sonatas, sonatinas, concerti, suites, and fantasias written in various styles from multiple genres to name a few. Sonatas are multi-movement pieces of music that follow a particular form called sonata form, and are usually accompanied by piano. Sonatinas are shorter sonatas. A concerto is a solo written to be accompanied by an orchestra. Suites are a multi-movement collection of dance tunes. And fantasias are music written to reflect improvisatory sounds, and do not follow particular parameters or forms like other music.

Solo recorder music will be where you work on your playing as an individual. Once you have started playing solo music fluently, you may wish to explore ensemble playing. In music, an ensemble is a group of musicians playing together. Duets are for two players, trios are for three, quarters are for four, etc. There is ensemble music written for various instrument combinations that include the recorder.

In the Renaissance and Baroque era, music for solely recorder groups was written frequently. A group of recorder players is often referred to as a consort. Recorder consorts mainly feature the sopranino, soprano, alto, tenor, and bass recorders.

Consorts can have multiple players on the same instrument, such as two tenor recorder players.

If you are interested in playing in a recorder consort or any ensemble, search for one in your area. Playing in an ensemble of any type is a great opportunity for musical growth and musical community.

Daily Exercises and Routines

Posture and Hand Position

Begin each practice session by setting up proper posture and hand position. Practice in front of a mirror to monitor your posture and hand position until it is habitual.

Posture Checklist

Standing

1. Feet shoulder width apart, body balanced equally between legs
2. Roll shoulders up, back, and relax
3. Keep back and neck tall, straight, and relaxed
4. Keep chin level with the floor
5. Bring the instrument to you

Sitting

1. Choose a sturdy chair that allows your feet to rest on the ground comfortably
2. Sit toward the front half of the chair, with your back away from the chair back
3. Place feet flat on floor in front of you
4. Roll shoulders up, back, and relax
5. Keep back and neck tall, straight, and relaxed
6. Keep chin level with the floor
7. Bring the instrument to you

Hand Position Checklist

1. Left hand is placed on top of recorder, with the right hand underneath
2. The left thumb covers the back tone hole, number 0, and the index, middle, and ring finger belong to tone holes 1, 2, and 3 respectively. The left hand pinky is not utilized
3. The right thumb is placed behind tone hole 4 for support on the back of the recorder. the index, middle, ring, and pinky finger belong to tone holes 4, 5, 6, and 7 respectively
4. Keep elbows away from the body, but not too high
5. Wrists should be straight and relaxed, not bent at an angle

Breathing Exercises

Training the body to breath in preparation for recorder playing will improve your sound quickly. Remember that for recorder playing, only a moderate volume of air is needed. The goal is to master the inhalation technique and to control the rate at which you exhale. Do at least one breathing exercise before every practice session.

Breathe in as much as you can, sending the air down low. As you breathe in, feel everything expand around your stomach and sides, keeping everything relaxed. Then, slowly exhale for as long as you can keep the air flowing
Inhale for 4 counts, hold for 4 counts, exhale for 4 counts, and hold for 4 counts
Relax your body, exhale your breath, and take a quick breathe without getting tense. Keep the throat open and expand from the diaphragm.
Take a deep breath and play a mid-range note for as many seconds as you can
Play a three note pattern ascending and descending all in one breath without articulating. Try repeating the pattern several times. Pick new notes at different pitch levels each day.

Rhythm Exercises

On the following page, there are ten rhythm exercises arranged in order of difficulty. It is recommended to use a metronome set to a slow tempo initially to keep your beat steady. These rhythm exercises can be practiced by clapping, singing/chanting, humming, tapping and also played on your recorder. Here is a suggested sequence in which to approach each exercise:

1. Count aloud and tap/clap
2. Sing/chant the exercise on a neutral syllable, such as "du" while keeping count in your head
3. Play the exercise on a single, mid-range note on your recorder
4. Play on various notes with your recorder
5. Increase the speed on your metronome for a challenge

Rhythm Exercises
for any recorder

Exercises and Songs for Recorders in "C"

The following exercises are for Recorders tuned in "C", such as the soprano and tenor recorder. If you play a recorder tune in "F", you may skip forward to the next section for exercises for your instrument.

Long Tones

It is recommended to start the playing portion of your practice session with slow, long tones to get the tone centered and breath pressure started. Choose any one of the following long tone exercises once you've established your posture and hand position.

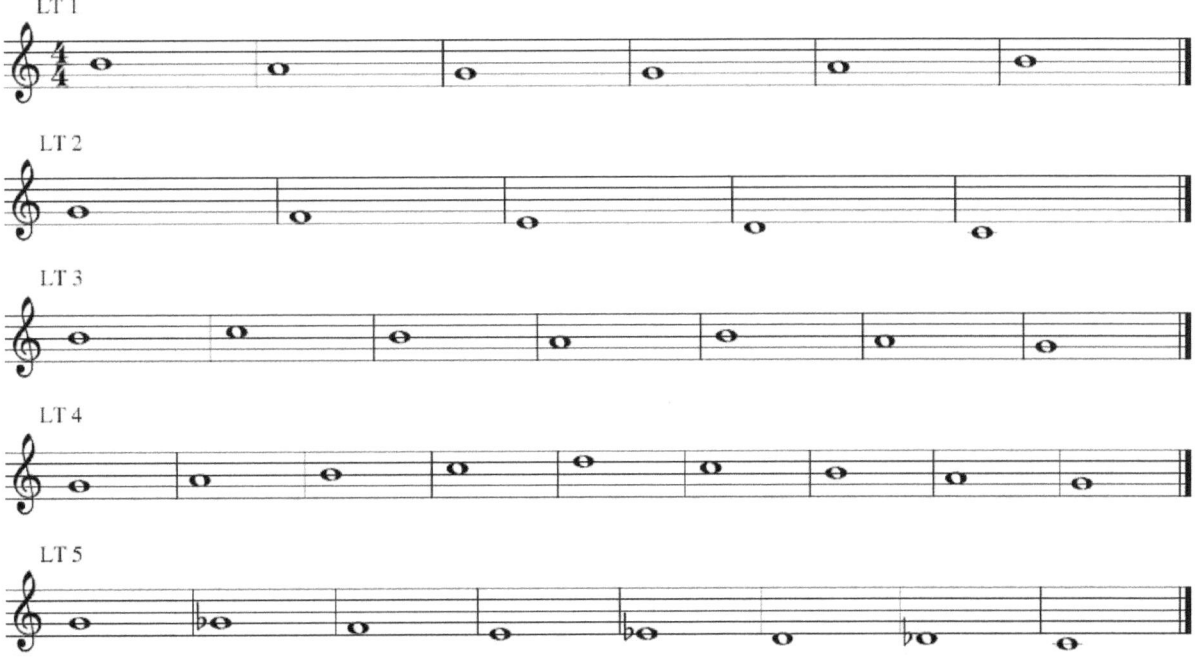

Preliminary Songs

These short folk songs are easier for any beginner to start making music. Here is a suggested approach to learning new music.

1. Check the time signature and key signature before starting any song (these preliminary songs do not have a key signature)
2. Count and clap/tap the rhythms at a steady, slow tempo. A metronome will assist
3. Chant or sing the letter names of each note in rhythm while fingering along on the recorder
4. Play the music

Songs for Recorder in "C"

Major and Minor Scales

These scales are in ascending order number of sharps or flats, adding accidentals to the key signature as you progress to the next scale. It is best to start by mastering the major and/or minor scale of the music you are currently practicing. For the recorders in "C", the C Major scale is the suggested scale with which to begin.

Regular review of each scale will allow the fingers to build muscle memory. It is vital that you check the key signature before starting each scale. The major scales are on the lift, with their parallel (share the same key signature) minor scales on the right side. The minor scales featured here are in harmonic minor form, with the seventh note of the scale raised a half step. You will see this marked with an accidental in every minor scale included below. Harmonic minor is the most commonly used form of minor. If you are interested in studying scales beyond those included in this guide, there are various scale method books available for purchase from most music retailers.

At first, practice each scale with a "du" tongue without any increase or decrease in dynamic. Once a scale has been mastered, spice it up by varying the articulations and dynamics.

Practice each scale at each dynamic level. As a reminder, to play softly, leak a finger, and to play loudly, shade a finger. If you master this, try getting gradually louder as you ascend on the scale (crescendo), and getting gradually softer as you descend on the scale (diminuendo). If you're feeling really adventurous, try the inverse as well!

The yellow box below and to the left contains suggestions of how to vary tongued vs. slurred patterns. "Slur four" or "slur two" mean to add a slur to the specified number of notes in a group. Each tongue/slur pattern is also pictured below the boxes.

You can also practice the various articulation styles on these scales once you've mastered the notes and fingerings.

Tongue/Slur Patterns

1. Tongue all
2. Slur four
3. Slur two, tongue two
4. Tongue two, slur two
5. Slur two, slur two
6. Slur three, tongue one
7. Tongue one, slur three
8. Tongue one, slur two, tongue one

Tongue/Slur Patterns

Articulation Styles

1. Generic "Du" tongue
2. Staccato "Dot"
3. Staccatissimo "Dit"
4. Accent "Tah"
5. Marcato "Tit"
6. Portato "Lu"

Articulation Styles

Major and Minor Scales
for Recorder in "C"

Exercises for Recorders in "F"

The following collections of exercises are for Recorders tuned in "F", such as the sopranino, alto, and tenor recorder. If you play a recorder tune in "C", use the exercises found in the preceding section.

Long Tones

It is recommended to start the playing portion of your practice session with slow, long tones to get the tone centered and breath pressure started. Choose any one of the following long tone exercises once you've established your posture and hand position.

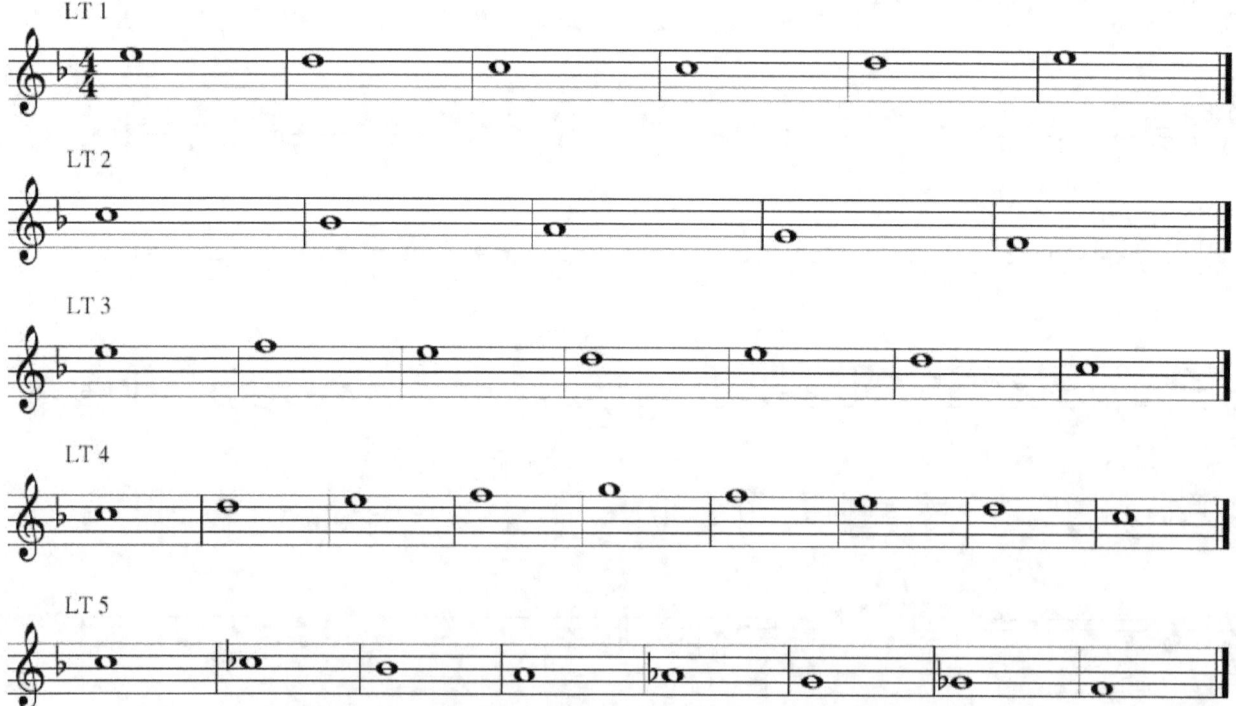

Preliminary Songs

These short folk songs are easier for any beginner to start making music. Here is a suggested approach to learning new music.

1. Check the time signature and key signature before starting any song. Also check for accidentals (flats and sharps attached to notes) throughout the music. These preliminary songs use accidentals rather than any key signatures.
2. Count and clap/tap the rhythms at a steady, slow tempo. A metronome will assist
3. Chant or sing the letter names of each note in rhythm while fingering along on the recorder
4. Play the music

Songs for Recorder in "F"

Major and Minor Scales

These scales are in ascending order number of sharps or flats, adding accidentals to the key signature as you progress to the next scale. It is best to start by mastering the major and/or minor scale of the music you are currently practicing. For the recorders in "F", the F Major scale is the suggested scale with which to begin.

Regular review of each scale will allow the fingers to build muscle memory. It is vital that you check the key signature before starting each scale. The major scales are on the left, with their parallel (share the same key signature) minor scales on the right side. The minor scales featured here are in harmonic minor form, with the seventh note of the scale raised a half step. You will see this marked with an accidental in every minor scale included below. Harmonic minor is the most commonly used form of minor. If you are interested in studying scales beyond those included in this guide, there are various scale method books available for purchase from most music retailers.

At first, practice each scale with a "du" tongue without any increase or decrease in dynamic. Once a scale has been mastered, spice it up by varying the articulations and dynamics.

Practice each scale at each dynamic level. As a reminder, to play softly, leak a finger, and to play loudly, shade a finger. If you master this, try getting gradually louder as you ascend on the scale (crescendo), and getting gradually softer as you descend on the scale (diminuendo). If you're feeling really adventurous, try the inverse as well!

The yellow box below and to the left contains suggestions of how to vary tongued vs. slurred patterns. "Slur four" or "slur two" mean to add a slur to the specified number of notes in a group. Each tongue/slur pattern is also pictured below the boxes.

You can also practice the various articulation styles on these scales once you've mastered the notes and fingerings.

Tongue/Slur Patterns

1. Tongue all
2. Slur four
3. Slur two, tongue two
4. Tongue two, slur two
5. Slur two, slur two
6. Slur three, tongue one
7. Tongue one, slur three
8. Tongue one, slur two, tongue one

Tongue/Slur Patterns

Articulation Styles

1. Generic "Du" tongue
2. Staccato "Dot"
3. Staccatissimo "Dit"
4. Accent "Tah"
5. Marcato "Tit"
6. Portato "Lu"

Articulation Styles

Major and Minor Scales
for Recorder in "F"

Listening Suggestions

Recorder Virtuosos

Abreu, Aldo

Adams, Piers

Antonini, Giovanni

Begley, Rachel

Boeckman, Vicki

Bosgraaf, Erik

Brüggen, Franz

Holtslag, Peter

Kemp, Jill

Lacey, Genevieve

Laurin, Dan

Leenhouts, Paul

Linde, Hans-Martin

Maute, Matthias

Oberlinger, Dorothee

Petri, Michala

Solomon, Ashley

Steger, Maurice

Van Hauwe, Walter

Verbruggen, Marion

Recorder Ensembles

Amsterdam Loeki Stardust Quartet

Flanders Recorder Quartet

The Royal Wind Music

Quartet New Generation

Seldom Sene

Composers of Recorder Music

Medieval (c. 500-1400)

Ciconia, Johannes

Renaissance (c. 1400-1600)

Fontego, Silvestro Ganassi dal

Gervaise, Claude

Holborn, Anthony

Praietorius, Michael

Senfl, Ludwig

Susato, Tielman

Baroque (c. 1580-1750)

Bach, Johann Sebastian

Bertali, Antonio

Boismortier, Joseph Bodin de

Hottetterre, Jacques-Martin

Purcell, Henry

Schickhardt, Johann Christian

Telemann, Georg Phillip

Quantz, Johann Joachim

Van Eyck, Jacob

Classical (c. 1730-1820)

Bach, Carl Phillip Emanuel

Krahmer, Ernst

Sammartini, Giuseppe

Modern/Contemporary/Neo-Baroque

Staeps, Hans Ulrich

Zahnhausen, Markus

Recorder Websites

American Recorder Society:
https://americanrecorder.org/

Society of Recorder Players:
https://www.srp.org.uk/

Baroque Recorder in C – Fingering Chart

*This note requires closing the bell of the recorder with the knee

Baroque Recorder in F – Fingering Chart

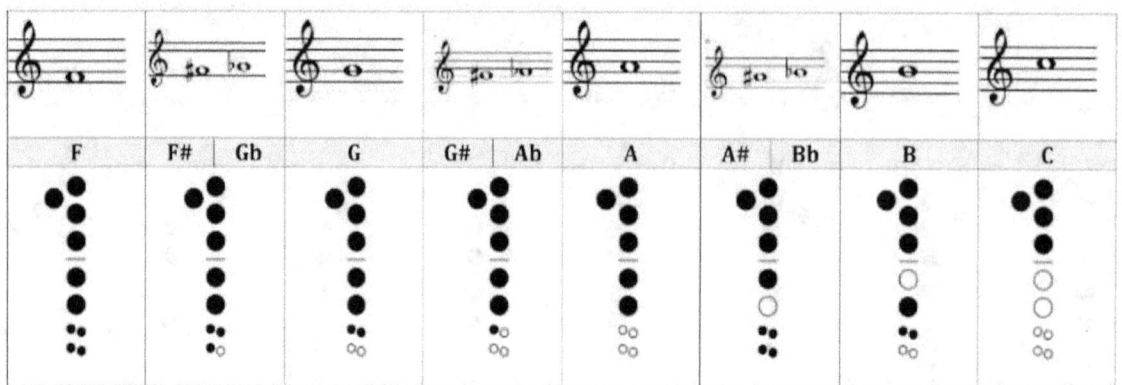
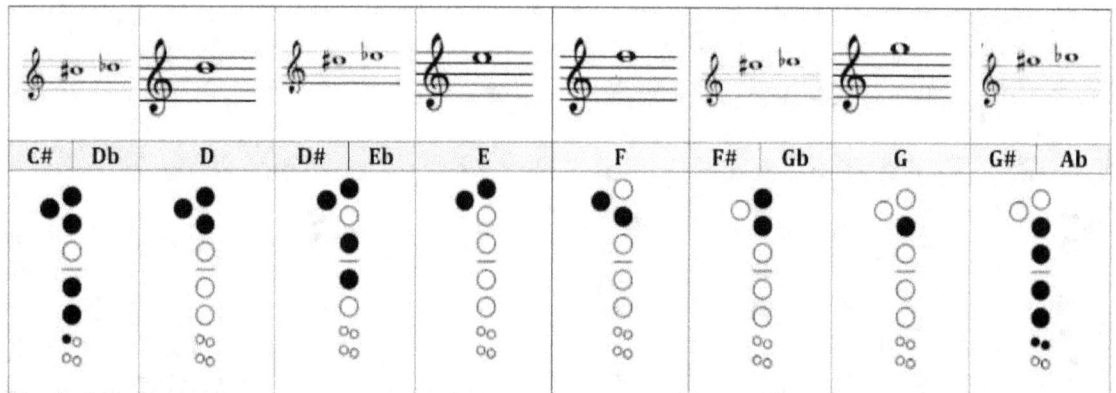
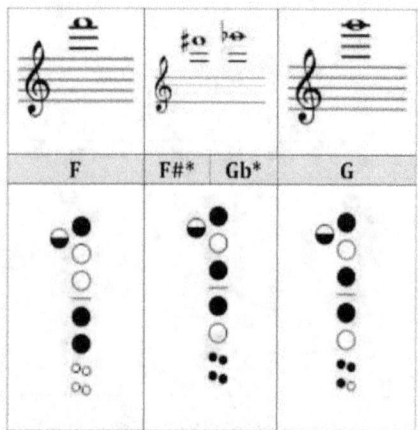

*This note requires closing the bell of the recorder with the knee

Afterword

Congratulation on reaching the end of the book! By now, you should have a strong grasp of the basics of learning how to play the recorder. While there is much, much more to learn about the instrument, and music as a whole, this guide will have left you equipped to go on to the next project with confidence. I encourage you to use this guide as a reference tool whenever you may need to reacquaint yourself with a term or symbol. Re-reading it may prove useful as well, when you feel you need a refresher. The following pages include all of the terms and symbols analyzed throughout the guide with page numbers and a brief description for quick reference. Thank you and best wishes as you continue your musical endeavors!

Glossary of Musical Symbols

Notes and Rests
Whole Note - 𝅝
Whole Rest - 𝄻
Half Note - 𝅗𝅥
Half Rest - 𝄼
Quarter Note - ♩
Quarter Rest - 𝄽
Eighth Note - ♪
Eighth Rest - 𝄾

Musical Structure
Treble Clef - 𝄞
Common Time - 𝄴

Staff -	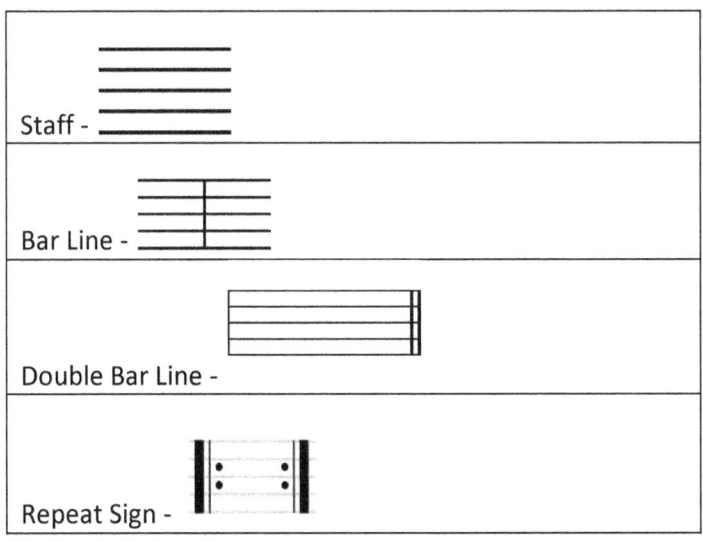
Bar Line -	
Double Bar Line -	
Repeat Sign -	

Dynamics, Articulation and Expression

Crescendo -	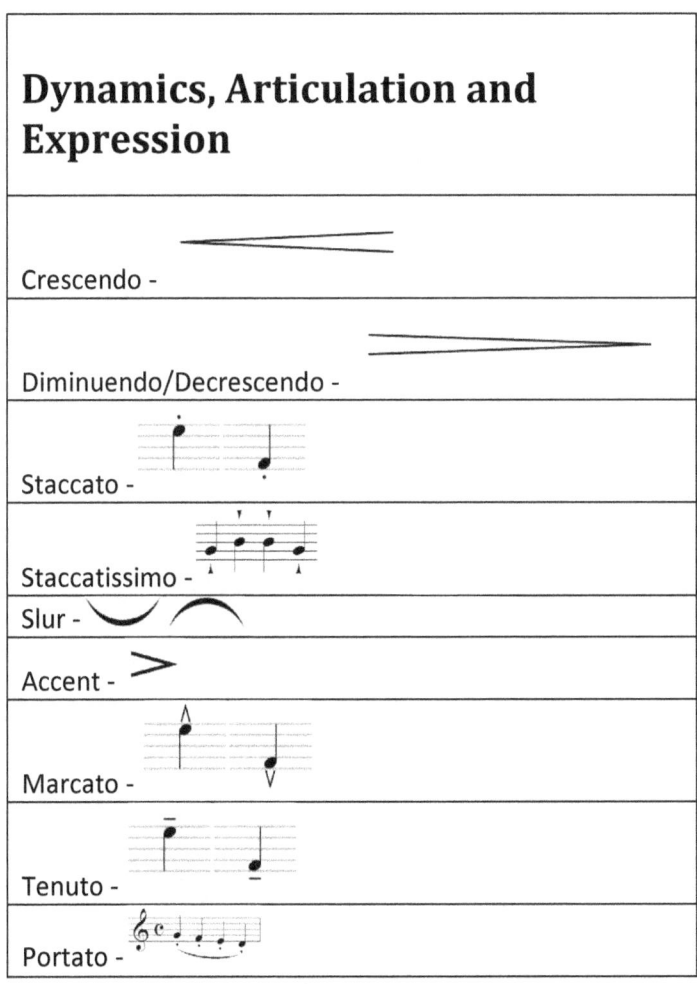
Diminuendo/Decrescendo -	
Staccato -	
Staccatissimo -	
Slur -	
Accent -	
Marcato -	
Tenuto -	
Portato -	

Alterations, Ornaments, and Other Markings

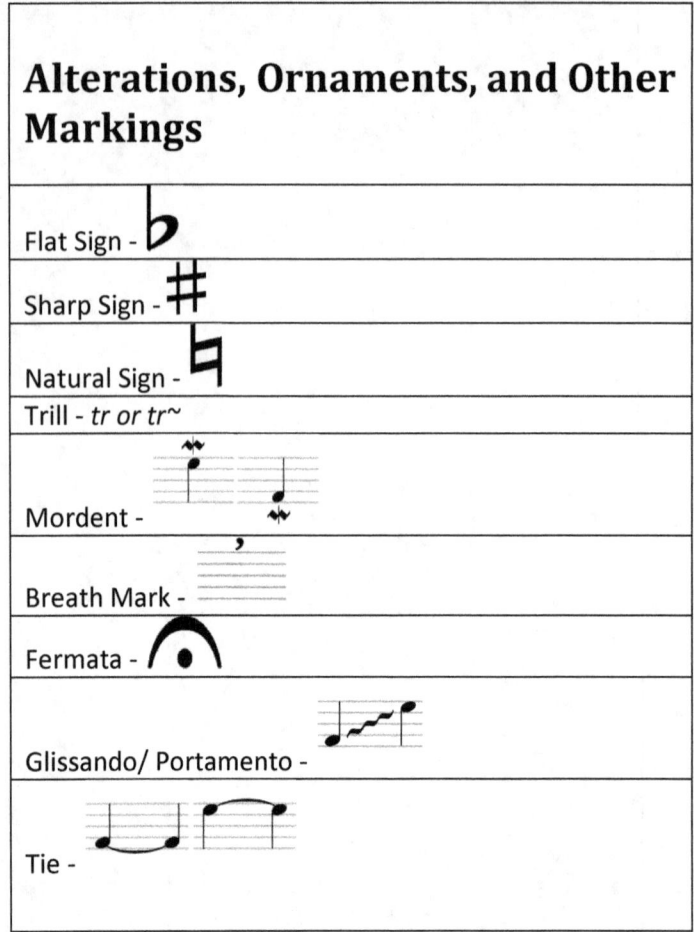

Glossary of Musical Terms

Accent (Page 65) - an articulation marking that indicates emphasis or a stronger attack to the note or notes to which it is attached

Accidental (Page 59) - a flat, sharp, or natural sign attached to a note that is not in the key signature

Alto Recorder (Page 4) - an instrument of the recorder family, tuned in "F", also known as a treble or consort flute

Anacrusis (Page 25) - one or more notes before the first measure of a piece of music

Articulation (Page 11) - how a note is approached or attacked, and on the recorder, with the tongue

Bar Line (Page 24) - a vertical line used to separate music into measures

Barrel (Page 7) - the center section of a recorder

Bass Recorder (Page 3) - an instrument of the recorder family, tuned in "F", and plays an octave lower than the alto recorder

Beak (Page 7) - a part of mouthpiece of the recorder, at the top, where the lips are placed

Block (Page 13) - a removable insert of wood on which your lower lip rests on the recorder

Bore (Page 13) - the inside of the middle of the recorder

Breath Mark (Page 28) - an apostrophe marking that indicates where to breathe in the music , usually placed in order to support musical phrasing

Circle Of Fifths (Page 57) - a way of organizing the twelve pitch classes into a sequence

Chromatic (Page 38) - refers to a note that is not in the key of a piece of music. Often denotes an accidental

Cleaning Rod (Page 13) - a long, thin rod, often with an eyelet, that is paired with a piece of cotton and used to swab the moisture from the inside of some instruments

Common Time (Page 27) - an additional way to notate the 4/4 time signature

Consort (Page 55) - a group of recorders played together in an ensemble

Crescendo (Page 60) - a marking in music that indicates to gradually get louder

Decrescendo (Page 60) - a marking in music that indicates to gradually get softer

Diminuendo (Page 60) - an additional marking in music that indicates to gradually get softer

Double Bar Line (Page 25) - a thin, vertical line followed by a thick, vertical line indicating the end of a musical piece

Dynamics (Page 59) - the volume of the music in relation to loud and soft markings

Eighth Notes (Page 23) - a note with the duration of 1/8 of a whole note, which in most time signatures is 1/2 of a beat

Embouchure (Page 52) - the placement of the lips, facial muscles, tongue, and teeth to play a wind instrument

Enharmonic (Page 21) - two ways to spell or notate the same pitch

Ensemble (Page 55) - groups of musicians performing together

Expression (Page 59) - the art of playing or singing with a personal response to the music using dynamics, phrasing, articulations, and interpretation

Fermata (Page 28) - a marking that indicates to sustain the note for longer than its usual duration. This may be determined by a conductor or soloists

Flat Sign (Page 20) - a "b" like sign that indicates to lower a pitch by a half step or semitone

Foot Joint (Page 7) - the bottom portion of the recorder that hosts a tone hole and the bell

Glissando (Page 68) - a glide from one pitch to another

Half-holing (Page 38, 49) - a technique in which a finger partially uncovers a tone hole. Also see "leaking", "shading", and "pinching" for context

Half Note (Page 23) - a note with the duration of 1/2 of a whole note, which in most times signatures is 2 beats

Harmonic Minor (Page 57) - scale in the minor mode with the seventh pitch raised a half step. The most common form of minor scales

Head Joint (Page 7) - the top portion of the recorder, hosting the beak and window

Intonation (Page 54) - the pitch accuracy of a musician or musical instrument

Key (Page 55) - a group of pitches or scale that forms the basis of a musical composition

Key Signature (Page 55) - a set of sharps or flats grouped together near the clef on the staff that notates the key of the music

Labium (Page 8) - the flat, thin edge found inside the window where the sound of the recorder is created

Leaking (Page 59) - a technique used to play softly by slightly pulling a finger off of a tone hole to leak air in order to keep the pitch raised

Ledger Lines (Page 18) - short lines notated above or below the musical staff that extend the staff to include notes higher or lower than the main five lines

Legato (Page 64) - a musical style in which notes are played smoothly and connected. Often notated using a slur

Long Tones (Page 53) - long, sustained durations of notes often used in warm-up sequences

Major Scale (Page 55) - a sequence of eight notes that progress in steps within an octave

Marcato (Page 65) - an articulation marking that indicates a short, strong attack to the note to which it is attached

Measure (Page 24) - a segment of time within a piece of music that groups the music into a specified number of beats determined by the time signature

Melodic Minor (Page 57) - a form of the minor scale in which the descending pattern differs from the ascending pattern of steps within an octave

Meter (Page 24) - refers to the regularly recurring patterns and emphases that occur within a measure in relation to the time signature

Metronome (Page 22) - a device that measures the speed, or tempo of music using Beats Per Minute (BPM). Used as a practice tool to develop steadiness and speed

Middle Joint (Page 7) - the center section of the recorder, hosting most of the tone holes

Minor Scale (Page 55) - a sequence of eight notes that progress in steps within an octave

Mouthpiece (Page 7) - the top of the recorder where the mouth is placed

Mordent (Page 68) - a musical ornament or embellishment in which the note is played with a single rapid alternation with the note above or below

Natural Minor (Page 57) - a form of the minor scale in which none of the notes are altered

Natural Sign (Page 21) - a sign that cancels a flat or sharp sign and represents the unaltered pitch of the note

Octave (Page 16) - the interval of between one musical pitch and another of the same letter name, or pitch class

Ornaments (Page 66) - musical embellishments that are not essential to the overall melodic line, but serve to decorate the music

Pick-up Notes (Page 25) - notes before the first measure of a piece of music that "pick-up" into the song or musical composition

Pinching (Page 38, 49) - the technique of partially covering or uncovering the thumb hole to create higher notes on the recorder

Phrasing (Page 28) - the grouping and shaping of notes in a musical passage, often separated with a lift or breath

Portamento (Page 68) - like a glissando, to glide smoothly between notes.

Portato (Page 64) - notated using staccato markings under slurs, an articulated legato

Quarter Note (Page 23) - a note with the duration of 1/4 of a whole note. which in most time signatures is 1 beat

Recorder (Page 3) - a family of woodwind instruments in the group known as internal duct flutes, or fipple flutes

Repeat Sign (Page 28) - a double bar line paired with two stacked dots which indicates to repeat a song, line, or section

Rests (Page 24) - durations if silence that correspond in name with durations of sound, i.e. whole, half, quarter, and eighth

Rhythm (Page 21) - the placement of sounds in time

Rhythmic Dot (Page 26) - a dot to the right of a note that increases its duration by half of its original value

Scale (Page 35, 46) - a sequence of pitches

Shading (Page 38, 49) - a recorder technique in which the finger partially covers a tone hole in order to lower the pitch to compensate for blowing strongly to play loudly

Sharp Sign (Page 20) - a marking used to indicate a note to played a half step or semitone higher

Slur (Page 64) - a curved line used to indicate smooth, connected playing in a legato style

Sopranino Recorder (Page 3) - the second smallest recorder of the modern recorder family, tuned in "F"

Soprano Recorder (Page 3) - the most common size of recorder, tuned in "C"

Staccatissimo (Page 63) - an articulation marking that indicates a sharp, detached approach to the note

Staccato (Page 63) - an articulation marking that indicates a light, detached approach to the note

Staff (Page 17) - a collection of five horizontal lines and the four spaces between them used to notate pitches in music

Tempo (Page 22) - the speed of the music

Tie (Page 26) - a curved line used to combine two durations of the same pitch

Time Signature (Page 24) - the notation of the meter in music found at the beginning of a musical composition as two numbers stacked. The top number indicates how many beats are in each measure, the bottom number indicates what type of note receives the beat

Tenor Recorder (Page 3) - an instrument of the recorder family, tuned in "C", pitched an octave lower than the soprano recorder

Tenon (Page 13) - a projection at the joints of the pieces of recorder that inserts to join the pieces together

Tenuto (page 64) - an articulation marking that indicates a smooth, connected style with little separation by the tongue

Tone (Page 49) - a steady periodic sound, often used to describe the quality of sound

Tonic (Page 55) - the first note of a scale

Treble Clef (Page 17) - a symbol placed on every line of recorder music that shows which notes are assigned to the lines and spaces of the staff

Trill (Page 67) - a musical ornament or embellishment in which the note is rapidly alternated with the note above the indicated note

Tuner (Page 54) - a device used to measure intonation accuracy, or if a pitch is higher or lower than the desired frequency

Vibrato (Page 60) - the intentional and steady fluctuation of a pitch used to add expression in music

Whole Note (Page 23) - a note with the duration of 4 beats

Window (Page 7) - the small, square opening on the front of the mouthpiece of the recorder from which the sound is created like a whistle

Woodwind (Page 3) - a family of musical instruments within the category of wind instruments. played by blowing into its mouthpiece

www.ingramcontent.com/pod-product-compliance
Lightning Source LLC
Chambersburg PA
CBHW081346070526
44578CB00005B/742